A Criminal &
An Irishman

A Criminal &
An Irishman

The Inside Story of the
Boston Mob-IRA Connection

Patrick Nee
Richard Farrell &
Michael Blythe

STEERFORTH PRESS
HANOVER, NEW HAMPSHIRE

For information about permission to reproduce
selections from this book, write to:
Steerforth Press L.L.C., 45 Lyme Road, Suite 208
Hanover, New Hampshire 03755

The Library of Congress has cataloged the hardcover edition as follows:

Nee, Patrick, 1943–
 A criminal and an Irishman : the inside story of the Boston mob-IRA connection /
Parick Nee, Richard Farrell, and Michael Blythe. — 1st ed.
    p. cm.
ISBN-13: 978-1-58642-103-8 (alk. paper)
ISBN-10: 1-58642-103-4 (alk paper)
  1. Gangs — Massachusetts — Boston. 2. Nee, Patrick, 1943– 3. Gang members —
Massachusetts — Boston — Biography. 4. Irish American criminals — Massachusetts
— Boston. I. Farrell, Richard, 1957– II. Blythe, Michael. III. Title.

HV6439.U7M46 2006
364.106'60974461—dc22

ISBN-13 (PAPERBACK): 978-1-58642-122-9

FIFTH PRINTING

CONTENTS

AUTHOR'S NOTE

Not one account in this book is taken from a newspaper article, a police report, or somebody else's "gangster" book. Everything detailed in this book I have either done, seen done, or heard about from the person who did it.

Most reporters and authors who write Southie gangster books use CIs — confidential informers — as sources. However, seldom is the majority of information compiled by these sources correct information. Confidential informers are self-serving criminals who lie.

This book is different from other books on the Boston Irish mob or any other "Whitey/Southie" crime book. If my recollections don't match those in some other book by some other criminal, I don't care. My memory is not perfect. This is my life as I remember it. And I'm comfortable with that.

PATRICK NEE

1. HOW TO ROB AN ARMORED CAR

My mother always said that the biggest mistake she ever made in her life was not throwing me off the back of the *Britannic* as we crossed the Atlantic Ocean in 1952. She said it would have been very easy to pull off — me being so small, I would have hit that dark, cold blanket of water in the middle of the night and no one would have been the wiser.

"If only I had known, back then," she'd say. "If I had any notion you'd turn out to be a gunslinger, I would've saved your father and me a lot of headaches. If I could have seen the future, you would have been on the bottom of the Atlantic."

Warring is all I'm really good at. I was born in Ireland during World War II, came to America at the beginning of the Korean conflict, saw action in Vietnam as a U.S. marine, and fought in the Mullen-Killeen gang war for control of South Boston's underworld during the 1970s.

So it was only natural that I would take my military expertise back to my homeland and engage the enemy, the British.

Some might think I'm overstating my role in helping the IRA kick the English out of Ireland. Let me explain by beginning at the end: the day my role in the IRA's fight came to a conclusion.

Engaging the enemy was all I knew. That's why I decided to take down an armored truck on a suburban street outside of Boston. Military precision was the key to my success — or my complete failure.

You never hit an armored truck that has more than a driver and a messenger inside. I was the lead charger. My job was to surprise the driver before he stepped out of the truck and had a chance to react. I'd rip his gun out of his holster, force him back toward the driver's seat, stick a .357 Magnum in his ribs under his Kevlar vest, and give him the order to drive. Everything had to be perfectly synchronized. The two rear chargers had to startle the messenger before he could communicate with someone inside the bank, move him quickly inside the truck, and close the back doors at the same instant I ordered the driver to go. We had three to five minutes to snatch the truck, clear the area, and get the truck to a place where we could rob it "discreetly." We wouldn't want to rob a truck in full view of bank employees and passersby.

Like any other risky endeavor in life, the secret to a successful heist is proper planning. Proper execution is the result of doing your homework. If you do it well, nobody dies — and almost as important, everyone gets rich. The asshole robbers who kill guards needlessly are mostly whacked-out drug addicts. I was a criminal with a passion: to drive the British out of Ireland. I didn't want anyone to die needlessly in that pursuit.

I was born in Ireland and came to the United States as a kid. In my thirties I developed tremendous respect for the Irish Republican Army's mission. So I had two defined goals when I began robbing armored trucks. I wanted to continue helping the IRA get the English out of Ireland, and I wanted to acquire enough money to accomplish that goal. The way I saw it, the more money I had the more help I could give the IRA.

I had already been assisting the IRA in any way that I could. Since the early 1970s I'd been sending weapons to the freedom fighters in Ireland; in January 1989 I was released from Danbury Federal Correctional Institute after serving eighteen months for orchestrating the largest shipment of guns ever smuggled to Ireland. On September 29, 1984, acting on a tip-off, two Irish Naval Service ships seized a fishing trawler, the *Marita Ann*, some two hundred miles off the west coast of Ireland. Inside the hull they found 163 assault rifles, 71,000 rounds of ammunition, one ton of military explosives, a dozen bulletproof vests, rocket ammunition pouches, 13 military-surplus weapons, weapons manuals, and military operation manuals. My friends and I had amassed the 7.5 tons of weapons, valued at some $1.2 million — all slated for the IRA.

For seven months following my release from federal prison I sat in the Coolidge Halfway House on Huntington Avenue in Boston, just biding my time and being a citizen. In fact, while I was there I completed a sixteen-week class in Irish studies at the University of Massachusetts. That was the great thing about living in the halfway house: I had the freedom to attend classes with regular students at the Boston campus.

It was only a few months after I finished my stay at the Coolidge House that I jumped back into the service of the IRA. I got a call one evening that an IRA man needed to see me in Quincy, just south of Boston. When I got there he told me he'd spent the last six months looking up and down the East Coast for a list of desired handguns. For some reason he just couldn't put them together. I looked at the list and fought hard not to show that I was very, very pleased: I had every weapon the IRA needed.

It took me about an hour to gather them up. All I had to do was drive to South Boston and raid my private stash. Many of those guns belonged to James J. "Whitey" Bulger, the notorious South Boston mobster turned informer. Whitey loved being associated with the IRA and the cause of Irish freedom; it seemed to give him a sense of purpose. In raiding Whitey's cache there was satisfaction for me in knowing how much every IRA man who'd ever met Whitey distrusted him while Whitey sucked up to them and thought that being associated with them gave him some legitimacy. That was all the incentive I needed. Besides, every day I spent in Southie convinced me more and more that I had to pull away from Whitey Bulger.

There was just no way around it — Whitey was no good. He was a paranoid control freak with psychopathic and homicidal tendencies. Whitey clearly derived sexual pleasure from torturing and killing. He was smart and calculating, yes, but he was also a seriously sick fuck. Besides, by now I knew that Whitey Bulger was a rat; it was just a matter of time before the rest of the world knew it too. It just wasn't safe to be close to him anymore.

The IRA had come to Boston in the 1960s to explore the possibility of robbing banks and armored cars to support their cause. They'd been doing it in Ireland and England for years and they were interested in seeing if it would be easier to do in the States. Both Irish and British intelligence agencies had marked many of the IRA men and had even assassinated one of them, Larry McNally. With those IRA men out of the picture, and with the criminal scene in Southie having changed so drastically since my release from prison, I had to rethink the situation.

I decided to hold up armored trucks in order to send money to my IRA contacts. Clearly I had to balance the risk of getting caught with the potential for huge reward, along with the possibility of having to kill a guard, but I was confident that with the right planning, and more importantly the right guys, we could be successful.

There was one major obstacle, though. I wasn't an armored car man. I had to find guys who were. Mick McNaught, then forty-five, was an experienced IRA operative. And what experiences he'd had. I'd met Mick years earlier when I was running guns to the IRA; we called him Irish Mick. Mick loved Irish music, good food, and beautiful women. If you knew anything about Ireland, the instant you heard his brogue you'd know he was a Derry man. He was on the run, having left Ireland because he'd been targeted by British intelligence. Once the British Special Air Services know who you are and what they think you've done, it's best to leave town.

Mick and I had a few successful heists and had sent a good amount of money to the IRA already. Then we decided to pull a job at a bank in Lynn, Massachusetts. We'd been watching the place for over four months — it was a perfect set-up. Both guards were creatures of habit: they were always on time; neither ever removed their guns. The bank was downtown, surrounded by buildings that created natural cover, and the getaway routes were plentiful and accessible. But we needed another guy for logistics.

We approached Michael Habicht. Michael had so many complicated facets to him that not even a writer could invent him. He was thirty-three years old, German on his dad's side and Italian on his mom's, with dark, Mediterranean looks — tall and slim with a *GQ* sense of style. I always felt like I was wearing overalls when I stood next to Michael. He was a solid guy, a real old-school criminal: competent, vicious, and loyal to his friends. He was also an intense IRA sympathizer.

Michael seemed like a perfect partner, but once I approached him all our plans for the Lynn job were put on hold. Michael said he'd get involved but he needed our help first. He informed us that for the last three months he and three experienced partners had been planning a job at a Bank of New England branch in Abington, Massachusetts. They were short two guys. Mick and I were itching for something big, and Abington was bigger than Lynn. Michael was smart, loved what the IRA was doing, and — most importantly — I trusted him. He was one of those guys who immediately conveys solidness and loyalty. But what really convinced us was this detail: the armored truck would carry up to two million dollars. Michael said it was a six-man job. I was good at math; once I secured a promise from Michael that the IRA could have twenty percent of the take, Mick and I were in. Out of roughly two million dollars, the IRA would get $400,000 and each us would pocket over $260,000.

And here was the best part: Michael and his partners had

recently met someone who knew a guard on the Abington truck who said he could arrange a handover. The guard would get a cut too, and to everyone's great advantage. When you take the guards' itchy trigger fingers out of the equation, you increase the odds of success dramatically.

How could we say no?

The job satisfied my ultimate goals: money for the IRA and money for my lifestyle. Besides, Mick and I were both growing impatient for anything that would get our juices flowing again. We were both action junkies, looking for the thrill that comes from doing things that are risky as hell — and the cash that comes with them.

Michael and his crew had been watching the armored truck delivery to the Abington bank since September 26, 1989. On January 6, 1990, he asked us in; the job was set to go down just three days later. On the same day, the Federal Deposit Insurance Corporation declared the Bank of New England insolvent. Both the *Boston Globe* and the *Boston Herald* carried prominent stories concerning the bank's difficulties and the lengthy lines of depositors wanting to withdraw their funds. Michael figured the Bank of New England would be delivering larger amounts to each of its branch offices to cover the dramatic increase in withdrawals. He said they couldn't wait any longer. The time to hit the bank was now.

The only thing I didn't like, right from the get-go, was the lack of time I had to prepare. I had this churning in my gut. You always get anxious before a job, but something in this equation just didn't add up. Of course, the reminder that two million dollars was involved weighted the mental balance sheet real fast. Every job had its potential downside: somebody could get killed or you could get caught. But when you looked at it overall, the potential rewards of the Abington job far outweighed any consequences, especially when you weighed the handover aspect. If the job went as planned there would be no need for bloodshed — either for the guards or us. I couldn't pass it up.

I'd known the other three members of Michael's crew for years; they were seasoned criminals and sympathetic to the plight of Catholics in Northern Ireland. That's why my request for 20 percent going to the IRA was so readily accepted. Bobby Joyce, thirty-seven, was a serious man and a fierce street fighter who owned a "bucket-of-blood bar" in Dorchester. Jimmy Melvin, at forty-eight a year older than me, owned a nightclub in Boston. He was an upbeat, robust guy with a vicelike grip. He was also a good family man; he was always talking about his kids and how well they were doing in school and sports. Jim Murphy was forty-eight; the most memorable thing about him was this weird tic he had with his tongue. He'd be talking straight at you and suddenly he'd squish up his face and jet his tongue out like a frog chasing flies. Mick and I didn't like or trust Murphy much. It wasn't that we'd thought he'd rat us out or anything, he was just so weird!

Jimmy Melvin and the boys had done their homework. That's the monotonous part of sticking up an armored truck. The first thing you've got to do is watch the truck's delivery schedule for three to six months. You watch for weaknesses; you watch and study habits. Do the guards keep the safety strap on their holsters snapped? Does the driver unsnap his, or do they take their guns out of their holsters and carry them? You've got to know these details. The slight difference between snapped or unsnapped safety straps changes your entire approach. And if the guards carry their guns in their hands, you fold it up and find another truck to scout.

It's their attitudes that you're studying. Guns carried in their hands means they're frosty, wired up, looking and ready for trouble. Usually it's the younger guards who approach their deliveries this way. The older guys who haven't experienced a robbery in years — or maybe ever — they're usually laid back, sloppy.

When you see those young bucks, bright eyed and with comically fierce expressions on their faces, and they have their guns out, you think, "Let's find something easier."

The ideal situation is a bank on a corner with a street that runs along two sides. Conditions are perfect when you have that right angle. The armored truck pulls up on the left side. You park and get set up on the right, out of their sight. With the bank building itself forming a natural hiding place for your vehicle, the guards don't see you until you charge. But you have to be very careful when you scout. The FBI watches videotapes of these deliveries. They can spot familiar vehicles and familiar faces. Scouting is an art; in fact, it's probably 90 percent of the crime. Scout it right, plan it right, do it right, and you will make a lot of money.

Michael Habicht and his guys had actually videotaped a delivery to this Bank of New England branch. Jimmy Melvin had driven a stolen van to a strategic parking place across from the armored truck's delivery spot. A video camera was mounted inside the side window of the van. Jimmy got out of the van and went shopping in Abington while the camera recorded the entire two hours prior to the delivery. The tape showed us everything in living color. It was the perfect tool to prepare for the most critical moment — the charge.

The day before the job Irish Mick and I met up with the boys in Quincy. The six of us drove to Abington in final preparation. We spent eight hours running the plan, detailing it to the exact second. We drove the route until it became second nature. The bank was not situated on a corner; it was not an ideal location. Abington was a rural community and most of the businesses were in strip malls or were sparsely scattered along Route 139. Jim Murphy had borrowed his daughter's car, and even though Mick and I didn't like him, we trusted his skill. He was a master at escape routes.

"Do state police patrol this highway?" I asked.

"No. The nearest barracks are miles away," Murphy responded.

Mick jumped in. "Michael, how about the locals. Is there a pattern?"

"Yep, the police cruiser has been spotted most days on the other side of town getting coffee. The guy is pretty habitual," Habicht said.

Jimmy Melvin and Michael had studied the area for months. You had to plan for any possible situation. There could be no surprises. Anything left to chance could come back to bite you in the ass or shoot you in the chest. You needed to have at least one alternate escape route. It was all about procedure.

"Well, well, will you look at that," Mick suddenly pronounced with a deep grin. He'd spotted a beautiful young lady near our bank. She had long blonde hair and a clearly defined figure. His talk seemed to get thicker whenever women were involved. "That prick," I used to think, "what an advantage that enviable brogue gives him." "I can't figure out what they see in you, Mick," I shot back. "That mug of yours should scare the hell out of them."

Actually, Mick wasn't ugly at all, but he sure wasn't good looking as Irishmen go. Actually, he looked like he should be lecturing on logic or philosophy at some college. He certainly didn't fit the British stereotype of an IRA volunteer — a hard-hewn man with rugged features and a scally cap. Mick had an almost gentle appearance, although he was in fact far from gentle — he was a hardcore IRA operative.

"You're just jealous, Nee" he said with a devilish grin. "I've got women figured. I know what they want."

"What do they want, Mick?" Bobby Joyce asked curiously.

Did Bobby really believe Mick knew what women wanted? I wasn't sure.

"Sincerity. That's all they want. Sincerity."

"Sincerity! You've never been sincere a day in your life," I responded. Then I had to amend that, because Mick had demonstrated his sincerity as an IRA volunteer, with all the hardships and dangers that entails. "At least when it comes to women!" I corrected.

We all laughed.

By now the tension of the day's preparations was beginning to subside. All of us began to turn down the intensity a notch, except maybe for Habicht and Murphy. That was just their personalities. They both were great at their jobs but they handled the stress differently. Me, Mick, Jimmy, and Bobby used humor to release the anxiety.

The twilight was coming on hard. The air rushing in the front window was cold and biting. It definitely felt like snow.

"Nee, you got one problem." Mick paused. "Well, you've got more than one problem, but as far as women are concerned, you've got one big problem."

I couldn't help but laugh, and I couldn't respond because I had a hunch which bullshit line was coming next. Joyce and Melvin were laughing too. Mick savored his moment, and then sprung his insight on us.

"You're shallow." He chuckled. "They can sense it. Ah, yes, don't ya think they know you're only after a one-night stand? That ya don't care about their needs? Ah, Patrick, you're only foolin' yourself, because you certainly aren't foolin' them!"

Melvin, Joyce, Mick, and I laughed hard. Habicht and Murphy were flat, still serious and stiff. After a few moments, Murphy felt the need to put a stop to the laughter.

"Let's get home and get some sleep," Murphy blurted out. Even though I was irritated — he just hated us being less uptight than him — I knew Habicht and Melvin had to be up before dawn to plant the "boilers," the stolen getaway cars. Everything was a go. We were as prepared as we were ever going to be.

As we'd say in the Marines, confidence was high. Driving home there was a feeling of calm, powerful poise in the car. Mick leaned over to me and spoke softly and with a kind of measured assurance. "Patrick, tomorrow at this time we'll all be rich and Margaret Thatcher will have a few more sleepless nights."

The bottom line of a successful take is this: You can plan, detail, and discuss how you're going to react for hours. Everything always looks good on paper, and talk is just talk. But when the adrenaline is surging through your body like the fuel in a racecar at Indy, the only thing that matters is your response to action at that moment. When it comes time for execution, for getting the job done, it's all about the men you're working with. Will they do the right thing at the right time? Are they solid, confident guys, or are they weaklings, cowards who collapse when the deed needs to be done? What are you going to do when the guard reaches for his weapon? After you shout at him to freeze and he doesn't, what will you do? Shoot him down? Kill him? All that "he's-a-family-guy-with-a-job" shit has to be sorted out in your mind already. If he puts himself in harm's way, he accepts the consequences. Or he should. It's not about what the guard deserves. Of course he doesn't deserve to be killed. But in doing this particular job he accepts that his truck might get robbed, and that he might have to kill a robber — or be killed by us. I know that normal folks — "citizens," as we call them — find this hard to understand, but what I've been doing all my life is hard to understand. I am a criminal. By definition, we live outside society's bounds.

Anyway, I was determined to charge this armored truck, thrust my .357 Magnum in the driver's ribs, and calmly, but with authority, make sure he did exactly what I told him. But first I'd have to endure the wait. I'd had the same experience as a marine: the life-threatening situation, planning for the ambush, getting in place for it, and then the wait. Most of the same conditions were present in Abington that were present in Vietnam except for one — I was no longer in the service of the U.S. government. I'd seen combat in 'Nam, fought Whitey Bulger in a gang war, and had succeeded in countless risky criminal actions. I was confident the Abington job would go well.

I spent most of the early morning hours pacing my living room. The tension felt like a large elastic band squeezing my lower belly. I stood. I sat. I paced. And I listened to the clock, each tick a reminder of our impending assault on an armored truck with two million dollars inside. I played and replayed in my head each detail of the heist as we'd planned it, frame by frame, as if it were a movie. I'd left Danbury ten months ago. Would this be the last morning of my freedom, or the first day of my new life as an armed robber in service to the IRA?

During the night the snow had begun to fall, and by morning a thin white blanket covered the windshield of my car. Mick and I left South Boston right at 6:05 A.M. With traffic and the snow, we had about a forty-five minute drive ahead of us. I parked my car in Randolph, a safe location miles from Abington. Jimmy Melvin picked us up there in a red Dodge Caravan they'd stolen in December and stashed in a safe garage until we needed it.

Jimmy was never late. He was always dependable, solid, immovable. That's what made him a great partner and a great driver. If the shit went down, he'd be there waiting for you. He'd never leave anybody behind, even if something went wrong and shots were fired at him. And when you're doing the kinds of things we were doing, a guy like that is gold.

Michael Habicht and Jim Murphy had strategically parked two boilers in the vicinity of the bank earlier that morning. Then they picked up Bobby Joyce and met us at Trucchi's Market on Route 139, across the street from the bank. There was no problem parking in Trucchi's lot that early. Bobby transferred into our vehicle and took his position on the floor behind me. Habicht and

Murphy would spot for us at a safe distance across the street from the bank. Inside their vehicle they had a Motorola walkie-talkie and a police scanner tuned to the local frequency. We'd be focused on hitting the armored truck; they were our eyes and ears to the outside world.

We were set up and ready to go by 9:15. The snow had picked up and was beginning to stick to the streets. Jimmy Melvin had removed the rear seat from the Dodge Caravan. I was in the front seat with a pistol on my lap. Mick and Bobby were lying on the floor behind us. They had all the weapons and were prepared to charge. When I looked back at these solid men, I felt confident this was going to come off.

The armored truck had always arrived without fail by 9:30, but with the snow we naturally anticipated a small delay. We would wait in the rear of the parking lot until Habicht saw the armored truck pull up beside the bank. He'd wait until the messenger got out of the truck and opened its back doors. The instant he saw the driver inside the truck through the open back doors he'd bark the go over the walkie-talkies.

Nobody spoke. Nobody was scared. We all knew what we had to do to succeed.

Melvin looked like a picture out of the Roaring Twenties. He wore a short, dark car coat and a porkpie hat tilted slightly on his head. I was dressed in a black lightweight jogging suit over a white shirt and tie. Mick was dressed similarly, except he wore a sport coat under his jogging suit and had three pairs of handcuffs for the guards hanging from his belt. Bobby Joyce was wearing multiple layers of clothes, including a lightweight outer raincoat over work clothes and rubbers over his work boots. We planned to strip off the outer layer of clothing after the initial charge and takeover of the truck; that way we wouldn't fit the description given to the police. Each of us had dark wool pullover caps with eyeholes cut out and two pieces of duct tape that firmly attached our gloves to our sleeves. DNA testing was in its infancy; no way did we want to leave even a piece of hair behind.

By 10 A.M. I was beginning to get a little impatient. Something must have gone wrong. But maybe it was just the weather that was holding things up. I rolled my window down so I could feel the snow hit my face. I watched the flakes melt on my running suit. We couldn't sit here much longer. The Caravan contained an out-and-out arsenal. Mick had an Uzi semiautomatic pistol that had been modified to fire fully automatic at a rate of 600 to 700 rounds per minute. Bobby Joyce had two weapons: the first was a powerful .223 Remington rifle with a sawed-off stock and the second was a Mac-10 machine gun. The Mac-10 was equipped with a silencer. The mere possession of these weapons could put us behind bars — twenty years apiece for each weapon. It was far too risky to sit in a parking lot with this kind of weaponry.

Michael Habicht's voice crackled over the walkie-talkie. "I'm gonna look around. It's 10:30. Things don't feel right."

"I think we should end this right now, Jimmy," I said to Melvin.

"Habicht's good. He'll take a look and call it," Jimmy responded.

Then it hit me. I don't know where it came from. I'd been so enthusiastic about the handover idea that I'd neglected to ask who'd given the information to us. Plus, I'd trusted these guys; I trusted their judgment. Maybe it was the sixth sense you acquire when you become a seasoned criminal; I just knew something bad was going down.

"I don't like it," Habicht barked in. "Too many suits in the area. I'm gonna make one more pass and call it."

"Hey Bobby, how'd you come on to this job?" I asked.

"A friend of mine from Dorchester had an inside," he answered.

I snapped my head around like an owl. A chill went up my spine.

"Not Davie Ryan?" I ventured.

"Yeah. How did you know?"

Now I felt sick. "We're fucked," I announced. "Davie Ryan is a rat. We gotta get out of here NOW."

Tension exploded inside the van. Melvin opened his door and began to slowly walk away. Two late-model Ford LTDs instantly jumped into my view. We had no time to react. Suddenly Melvin was on his knees with a shotgun to his head. I slid my gun gingerly off my lap and between the seats the second I saw the FBI agent running toward me with a shotgun held chest high.

"They got us. Don't move," I said. I didn't want to see any of these guys get killed.

The shotgun fed was at the front windshield in a flash; he raised the gun to my face and yelled "Put your hands up." There was nothing I could do. I looked square into the barrel. It was six feet from my nose. The guy was thirty-something; the gun barrel shook up and down with his heavy breathing. I moved my hands slowly toward the window. This guy was so pumped; one tiny move would have turned my gray matter into soup.

There was no way out. I was going to jail for a long time. "Fuck!" was the only word I can recall thinking. Two strong hands ripped me out of the front seat. I was standing with my hands up when I felt an explosion hit the right side of my head just behind my ear. I went down. The left side of my cheek was forced into the pavement. I could feel the heel of somebody's boot cutting into the base of my neck. Everything was happening so fast. People were screaming and the only sounds I could clearly distinguish were the slapping of the rubber soles of FBI shoes hitting the pavement.

They sat us in a circle on the ground with our hands cuffed behind our back. When they pulled our hats off the FBI identified Melvin, Murphy, Habicht, and Joyce from Ryan's information, but they didn't have a clue about me or Mick. And I certainly wasn't going to tell them. I could hear them mumbling to each other, trying to figure out who the hell Mick and I were.

"That's Pat Nee," one of the Boston police officers yelled from the back of the circle of clustered federal agents.

Shit! If I had only gotten away nobody would have known I was in the car. Now I was going back to jail for maybe fifty years or more. My mind swelled with humiliation. Not at being on the ground or being caught, but at the thought of the food in the county jails where I'd be held until my trial, and the infamous federal bus tour I'd be on after my sentence: forced to ride for sixteen hours a day without stops for the bathroom, fed cheese and two-week-old bread, my ankles shackled and my hands secured tightly to my waist with a chain that acted as a belt. To drink water the guards would make you bite the tin cup and move your head back slowly to let the water trickle down your throat. Yes, my life was going to suck for a long time to come.

2. IRELAND

My family left Ireland for America in 1952, when I was eight. My recall of life Ireland comes from two sources: my memories and my imagination. My memories, of course, are sketches of events that I can see in my mind. But I was young, and after you've seen the things I've seen in my life, only prominent incidents survive in your mind. But the stories about Ireland that my mother and father told around the family table when we were growing up in America created a new set of memories, born both of my parents' recollections and my own imagination.

Our family had it tough in Ireland, sure, but I'm not going to tell you any of that *Angela's Ashes* crap to try to gain your sympathy. We might not have had many good clothes but Ma washed them every day. There was always good food. In fact, Ma never let my brothers and I go to bed hungry. And I remember falling asleep every night to a penetrating fire that burned until early morning.

Our people came from Rosmuc, a tiny village on the coast road northwest of Galway City, in the west of Ireland. We spoke Gaelic and we were separated by clans. Our people were called "Black Legs," because we had no shoes and our feet were always dirty. Back then people knew who you were by the clan you'd come from. My mother, Julia Grehlish, was from the Jude clan. My dad, Paddy Nee, came from the Padda clan. The clan name wasn't a name you'd use in marriage or in any other legal sense. It was just a way of distinguishing and recognizing families in Ireland.

My dad worked as a laborer in a cement factory just outside Galway City. Although he was only 5'10" with a medium build, he was rugged and his forearms were like sledgehammers. Dad had been in the Irish Free State Army — the army formed after the

Irish Free State Agreement of 1922 partitioned Ireland into Northern Ireland and what would later become the Republic of Ireland — before I was born. He was a nationalist to the very core.

In Rosmuc we lived in a white stone cottage with a thatched roof. Every night our entire family would sit together around the fire. My grandmother and grandfather, my six uncles, and Ma and Dad would tell story after story about Ireland's fight for freedom. I remember the fresh smell of burning turf filling my nostrils as my younger brothers — Peter, Sean, and Michael — slept sideways across one narrow bed. I'd watch the dark blue and orange flames dance into the darkness as the heat warmed my cheeks.

"There'll never be peace in Ireland until the English leave," Dad would say.

"For sure we'll get it back," Ma would reply.

As a kid growing up in Ireland I took for granted the fact that the British had stolen a piece of our country. Most of the songs my mother and father sang had something to do with getting our piece of land back from the British. But at eight years old I wasn't too sure what "getting it back" really meant.

Ma, the youngest of the Jude clan, was born in 1916. Everybody called her Baby Jude. One thing my mother never did was hold back a word she thought should be spoken. But it was not only her words that were strong; her presence cast a long shadow. She was statuesque — tall and dark with chocolate-brown eyes and pitch-black hair. The muscles in her back were thick and powerful from all the chores she'd done as a girl. The one thing I'll never forget about my mother was the size of her hands. She'd only have to make a fist and the thickness of it, with the protruding knuckles, would make you give a second thought to continuing your mischief.

When I was seven we moved to a row house on Courthouse Lane in Galway City. Dad told me years later that the economic conditions in Ireland were beginning to worsen then. Plants were closing down and new jobs were harder to come by. I guess it was at that time that Dad and Ma decided it was time to begin saving money for the boat ride to America. My father and mother wanted the very best for us kids and, sadly enough, it was becoming harder and harder to raise a family in Ireland.

The row houses in Ireland are the equivalent of what we in America call housing projects. Back then, most everybody in Ireland lived in row houses. If you live in a housing project in America you're labeled as poor and often feel humiliated. But the majority of people in Ireland were poor during the time I lived there. I never felt I was any different from anybody else. Nobody had more than we did and some had less. I had no idea what it meant to be poor.

There were no sidewalks in the section of Galway City we moved into. On Courthouse Lane, where we lived, the street ran right to the edge of the row houses. I remember the entire length of Courthouse Lane — identical stone houses painted white with dark brown ceramic roofs. The bottom floor of our house had a kitchen with a sink, running water, and a fireplace. There was no icebox. There was no toilet either; the outhouse was only a few steps outside the back door in our small, perfectly square backyard.

On the ceiling in the rear of the kitchen was a trap door that took you upstairs to a large loft. A thick green curtain divided the loft into two sleeping areas: Ma and Dad slept on one side while Peter, Michael, Sean, and I slept quietly on the other. Ma always opened the door early in the evening so the heat from the fireplace could warm the loft.

I have two vivid memories from our last months in Galway City, right before we emigrated to America. When it was time for me to begin school, Ma dressed me in the traditional Irish school uniform — a white shirt, knickers, and black shoes. I'd been to school in Rosmuc. Back there all the children were together in the same schoolhouse; my brothers and I studied Gaelic and English together. But here in Galway most of the schools were parochial — which meant, of course, that the teachers were nuns and brothers. I was in trouble in the Galway school before I ever sat down in my chair. And I think that was before I even opened my mouth.

You see, I am left-handed. I'll never forget one mean, ugly brother. He had to be six feet tall. His face was square, like a mailbox on an old country road. "I'll teach you to write with your left hand," he'd scream, as he pounded a wooden rod against the backside of my knuckles.

I think it took a week of Ma seeing my bloody knuckles at supper to change everything. At first she played it off; maybe she thought it would pass and that old Mailbox Head would stop his abuse. But each beating caused more bleeding and swelling. After five days I couldn't even clench a fist to do my chores. I wasn't able to carry turf into the fireplace anymore. For sure Ma wasn't going to settle for that.

I'll never forget how that old brother's face changed the day Baby Jude walked me through the front door and gave him a lesson in God's intentions. Ma squeezed those two big mitts of hers up close to the penguin's lips and quietly said, "God made my Paddy to write with his left hand. The next time young Paddy comes home with his knuckles beat up, I'll be back to separate the devil from you."

I never received the rod again for being left-handed. It's ironic, but from my very first day of Catholic school in Ireland trouble had a way of searching me out.

The other memory that still gets me laughing aloud today are the stories Ma and Dad used to feed me about the Tinkers that hung out on the corner of Courthouse Lane. Some people think the Tinkers of Ireland were nothing more than gypsies. But in fact the Tinkers not only helped the IRA, they played a significant role in building Irish nationalism.

The Tinkers were nomads who refused to settle in any one place. But unlike the Roma gypsies, many Tinkers owed their itinerant way of life directly to English rule. In the early 1500s a large swath of people refused to pay taxes to the English crown or to accept British law; they packed their belongings into wagons and moved about the country to escape the unjust Brits. Every time the Brits would get close to them they'd move out of their encampment in the middle of the night.

It's unfortunate, but as generations passed "Tinkers" became a derogatory epithet throughout Ireland. The Tinkers' nomadic lifestyle, combined with the staunch Irish Catholic beliefs of Irish society, unjustly turned the Tinkers into outcasts. So it was that the first people who refused to accept British law over time became disparaged and vilified by the Irish. At eight years old I was petrified of the Tinkers.

Down Courthouse Lane was a local pub that my dad would frequent on Fridays after work. Being the oldest, Ma would send me down to collect Dad's paycheck every Friday afternoon around five. I guess she was concerned Dad would get drinking and spend his whole check on pints of Guinness. He never once did, but Ma always sent me to grab his check before "the drink got him and spent the money."

I loved going to see my dad and listen for a time as he sang Irish fight songs with everybody else in the pub. But there was a serious consequence involved in my Friday afternoon routine, one that meant life or death to me. Without fail, I'd always have to confront one extremely onerous obstacle: the Tinkers. To be caught by them would surely be the end of me.

Every afternoon the Tinkers would stand on the corner of Courthouse Lane singing songs and dancing for money. The youngest and most fetching would always be right out front holding a small tin. Most Fridays they'd beg until well after dark. Of course, that created a big problem for me. It was my job to get to the pub, pick up my dad's check, and return home to my house without the Tinkers grabbing me and making me one of their own.

Ma and Dad had warned my brothers and me: Stay away from them; do not get even twenty feet within their reach. Everybody knew the Tinkers kidnapped little boys. Ma said that each and every little boy who held a tin cup was stolen from his family. She told me that only bad boys were taken away from their parents.

When it was time for me to go to Dad, I remember sneaking out the back door and slipping quietly through the backyards until I reached the alleyway. That was the opening, the place from which I'd have to run fifty feet or so to the pub's entrance. I'd stop at the alley doors and carefully peek up the narrow cobblestone street. There were the Tinkers. If they spotted me I'd never see my ma and dad again.

I inhaled a few times and then, as the butterflies flew wildly in my stomach, I just let my feet carry me. Sometimes it felt like running from a vicious dog nipping at your heels. Some folks claimed the Tinkers had magic powers. I believed it. It was spooky, as if you could always feel their presence right behind your ears. But I never turned back to see if they'd spotted me.

Back then, bowed legs and all, my little feet never failed me. I would hit the pub door and open it without breaking stride. Instantly the hair on the back of my neck would relax. Being inside meant perfect safety.

I would find Dad at his usual barstool. Every Friday he'd do the same thing: once my breathing returned to normal he'd pick me up, sit me on the bar, and give me a sip from his pint of Guinness. For a young kid this was worth the chance of getting caught by the Tinkers. I'd sip his pint and listen to Dad weave his stories. Every time he would finish a song or a story he'd toast Ireland. I forced small sips of the Guiness; I knew the last leg of my journey would be the most dangerous. As soon as my last taste was inside my mouth, Dad stuffed the check deep into my top pocket and picked me off the bar.

"Now be real careful of those Tinkers, Paddy. I heard they got two the other night on the outside of Galway. Your Ma needs that money. If the Tinkers get you, we'll never get that money back," Dad warned me, with a hint of a grin.

For sure, going back my life was in terrible danger. The Tinkers could see me. I had to run toward them. I remember opening the door slowly. I could hear my heart beat as I squeezed through the small entryway. The Tinkers couldn't see my first step. No way did I dare look up the street. I could hear them singing. Now was the time to make a break.

My feet hit the cobblestones like a dog on ice. Just then one of them would turn to see me. He had a straw hat on the side of his head and his clothes were weathered. I would see his smile just as my feet met the alleyway door. "I'm gonna get you one night," I heard his voice echo down the alleyway. The five or six backyards to my house all melted into one. I vaulted over each wall that separated the yards as if the walls didn't exist. Finally I ran through our kitchen door and turned over Dad's check to Ma. "Oh thank God," Ma said with a smile, "I thought for sure those Tinkers had taken the money."

Both Ma and Dad used the Tinkers to keep their kids in line. Most parents did. Of course, the Tinkers knew of our parents' warnings. They would play right along with the game and scare the daylights out of us.

My dad came to America in 1952. My mother's four sisters — Mary, Barbara, Ann, and Beatrice — had already emigrated between 1948 and 1951. All the sisters were single and came to America alone. Barbara, Beatrice, and Ann settled in South Boston while Mary moved immediately to Pittsburgh. Barbara had agreed to give my dad a place to live while he found work. Southie was rich with new Irish immigrants. It was a solid place for an Irishman to get a new start. Dad planned to save all his money and send us the fare to America.

In the months before my father took the journey across the Atlantic, Aunt Barbara had mailed a suit to Ireland. The plan was for Dad to wear the suit the day the ship docked in New York City. Nobody had cameras back in Ireland, so if you hadn't already met the person who was arriving, or you hadn't known them in Ireland, there was no way of telling who was who. It had been a long time since Barbara had seen my dad, and the next best thing to a photograph was clothes — Aunt Barbara would surely recognize the suit Dad was wearing. But my father wasn't one to wear something he was not fond of. He fancied himself a sharp dresser, and he hated the suit Aunt Barbara had sent. He said it made him look like an Englishman. He traded it for another suit on the boat across the Atlantic, then he walked the docks in New York City for hours waiting for Barbara to claim him. But that was Dad — a quiet, proud man.

He immediately got a job in the Laborers Union. They were Gaelic speakers. Every morning at 4:30 Dad would show up at the union hall in South Boston and wait. First to be called were the Irish immigrants who spoke Gaelic. Second to be called were the children of Irish immigrants. If you didn't fall into those two categories you were pure out of luck, because back then the Irish ruled South Boston.

It took Dad six months of hard labor to save enough money for our fare. One day I came home from school to find that Ma had dressed Peter, Michael, and Sean in their Sunday best. All of our clothes were neatly packed into two old brown leather suitcases. The row house was empty; everything we owned gone to other family members.

"Where we going, Ma?" I asked.

"To America, to see your dad," she replied.

I'd heard my parents talking about it before Dad left. I knew that someday we were going to go to America. But suddenly it was happening. Before I knew it my brothers and I were in a cab on our way to Cork.

I'll never forget the *Britannic*, the ship we came to America on. It was the biggest ship I'd ever seen in my life. It must have sat at least fifty feet out of the water. The sides were chocolate brown and the upper decks were tan. I remember how many lifeboats were tied to the top rail all the way around the ship. I can't remember if I'd ever seen that many people together in one place; I couldn't understand why so many of them were crying and hugging one another. I'm not sure how many people were on the ship, but going up the gangplank I felt like the cattle in Rosmuc being led to the pastures. I can't remember how I reacted, or if my mother and brothers were excited or frightened of the unknown. I just remember having an understanding that everything was about to change.

It took seven days to cross the Atlantic, and Peter and I never wanted to leave the ship. Sure, we were at the very bottom of the hull, in the cheapest cabin. But it was clean and if it weren't, Ma would have scrubbed it spotless. Ma thought it was great because the cabin had some things we didn't have in our houses in Rosmuc or Galway City, mainly a flush toilet.

The best part of our Atlantic crossing was the food. We'd never in our lives experienced a buffet — the food just wrapped around table after table and filled an entire room. The dessert tables were our favorite, with colors and sweets I'd never seen or tasted before. Peter and I loved this brown, creamy, sweet stuff that melted inside our mouths. One of the cooks told Peter it was called chocolate.

Poor Ma was seasick the entire crossing. The crew kept checking on her and brought soup that seemed to help her. I felt bad when the captain would make her come topside to get us. We were on a ship and it was a big ocean, so we fished, using my mother's yarn and a safety pin for the hook. Even though we never would have caught a bite, I guess the captain had rules about fishing off the back of the ship.

The day we entered New York Harbor, Ma, my brothers, and I stood on the top deck. I don't think anybody said a word for minutes. The sight of the city simply took your breath away. The buildings looked like paper drawings hanging from the sky. I'd never heard so much noise. I couldn't distinguish one sound from the other. They seemed to all blend together into the ship's loud horn signaling our approach. And the air in America smelled so different from Galway City. There wasn't the dampness or the penetrating dark cold that froze your nostrils. America! America! I was overwhelmed.

I spotted my dad first. His hand waved slowly back and forth; as we got closer I could see tears of joy filling up the corners of his eyes. Dad was with two ladies I didn't recognize, but after a few moments I could tell that one of them was my aunt Barbara. Although she looked quite different from the days sitting around a fire in Rosmuc, her hands and jawline resembled my mother's. The other woman, Mary Walsh, was young and beautiful. She was Aunt Barbara's daughter.

The first thing Dad wanted to do was eat. I'll never forget the first restaurant I ever went to in America. It was a roadside delicatessen just outside of New York City. And I'll tell you, it was nothing like the pubs of Ireland. I remember the waitress coming over to our table. She was wearing a uniform. I didn't quite know what to expect; she didn't look like any bartender I'd ever seen.

"What can I get you today?" she asked, in an accent quite different than mine.

"Paddy, what would you like?" Dad asked me.

I looked around the room trying to spot anything that would

give me a hint on what the hell I should order. It felt like the whole restaurant was quiet just waiting for me to respond. The waitress opened her eyes and slowly moved her pad of paper and pen closer to her chest. Suddenly Ma nudged me with her elbow.

"I'd like a pint and a herring," I blurted out in a thick brogue.

Nobody spoke. The waitress jerked her head upward. Suddenly, without any notice or reason, all the adults broke into deep, hearty laughter. It was infectious, the kind of laughter that grows each time somebody laughs anew. I looked around trying to figure out what they all were laughing at, and then I decided to laugh just so I wouldn't be the only one not laughing. Who knew they were all having a fit on my account? A pint and herring is exactly what we would have ordered in Ireland.

There were seven of us packed into Aunt Barbara's old Ford as we started the journey to our new home in South Boston. The eight-hour-plus ride to Boston was less than comfortable with so many people squeezed together. As we were leaving the restaurant parking lot Mary Walsh opened her black pocketbook and dug out a fist full of American coins, then turned them over to me as a gift. When it was my turn to sit by the window I began throwing the coins. I didn't quite know what to do with the money, and the newness of America's streets mesmerized me; I wanted to see how the coins would bounce off the pavement. There were fast cars racing down wide, open roads. Nothing in Rosmuc or Galway looked like this.

Sometimes I wonder what I would have become if I had stayed in Ireland. Would I have worked in a factory and raised a family the traditional Irish way? Would I have become a member of the IRA? I'll never know. But I do know one thing. In coming to America I found out the truth about America. It surely was the land of opportunity. I learned early on that in America anything was available to you if you wanted to work for it.

I also learned how easy it was to just take what you wanted. In America, crime pays very well. And like that lady standing in New York Harbor suggests, it's a free country — the perfect place for a criminal with ambition.

3. GUNSLINGER

Ma loved watching cowboy movies on Saturday after-
noons with Dad. For hours on end they'd sit in the living room
watching John Wayne westerns. Her favorite parts were the gun-
fights in the middle of the street. It was the tension, the standoff,
that held her, just before one would draw and the other one would
die. It was there in our living room that Ma decided to call me
Gunslinger. Something in her mind forced an association and,
whenever I made her angry, I became Gunslinger.

But I wasn't surrounded by violence at home. In fact, my life in
South Boston was quite calm and happy. For the first two months
we lived on the corner of G and Fourth with my Aunt Barbara's
family while Dad saved enough to get us our own place. I
remember the parties we'd have on weekends. They'd start on
Friday after the men got out of work and they would end early
Sunday morning, before church. All my Aunt Barbara's friends
wanted to come by and meet Ma and Dad. My brothers and I got
to meet our cousins for the first time.

At Aunt Barbara's we had three floors of living space with running water, a toilet that flushed from a metal chain connected to a
water-filled box on the wall, and most impressive of all an enormous free-standing bathtub that sat all alone in the middle of a
big, bright bathroom. Most of the time we spoke English, because
Aunt Barbara and Ma thought we should get accustomed to
American culture. But late into a Friday night party I would lie on
my bed listening to the wandering sound of Ma and Dad singing
Irish freedom songs in our old language. Even as a young boy I felt
safe hearing Gaelic songs filtering into the darkness of my bedroom. It kept Ireland close to me.

As much as I enjoyed the novelty of our new life in Boston, I missed our life in Rosmuc and Galway. Life in Ireland had always carried the rhythm of a reassuring routine: I'd wake up, go to school, come home, and do my chores. Ma would clean. When Dad came home we'd eat by the fire, Ma and Dad would sing and tell stories, and we'd be off to bed. But America was so strange. Everyday I'd be confronted with new material. The people looked so different and everybody talked funny. Instead of songs and stories, families sat around a box and watched shows on this thing called a television.

Early that summer we moved out of Barbara's house into our first apartment, on the corner of Third and Court Lane in South Boston. It was a small apartment; our bedroom was in the back of the house, and it had a toilet but no bathtub. But for a kid it couldn't have been a better neighborhood. The majority of the Irish who came to Boston automatically settled in Southie, following family members who had already emigrated. And too, South Boston might have reminded the Irish of Ireland; Southie was surrounded by water on three sides and insulated from Boston and outsiders by bridges.

Most of the houses in our neighborhood were triple-deckers — three tenements stacked on top of each other — and joined side to side by a shared wall that rarely blocked out the sounds of a good neighborly argument. No more than ten feet away from our front door was a grass field where my brothers and I played football; directly across the street was a perfectly square vacant lot bordered by a two-story brick wall running one entire side — a perfect site for stickball.

The gate to St. Bridget's Elementary School was less than fifty yards from my front door. Back then, before Judge Arthur Garrity's 1974 court decision that destroyed South Boston with forced busing, all kids went to school in their respective neighborhoods. St. Bridget's wasn't free. But Ma found a way to cut back on things around the house, clean a house here and there, and save to make the tuition. It was a given — all of her boys would receive a Catholic education.

But my mother's wishes for a fine parochial education for her sons didn't help me go quietly into St. Bridget's. I'll never be able to live down the first week of school. I didn't want to leave my house from the very first day. My mother had forced me to wear the traditional Irish schoolboy uniform, and she walked me the whole way up the street by the ear. I can still hear the sound of laughter as I waited to enter my classroom.

My mother didn't understand what the fuss was about. She thought I looked perfectly saintly with my new black shoes, white knee socks, three-button blue jacket over my white shirt and green tie, and tight beanie over the crown of my head. To this day I swear that even the principal smirked at my lovely getup.

I must have gotten into three fights at recess that first day. I was the only kid with a beanie and white knee socks in the entire school. And what made my plight progressively worse was the fact that I was destroyed in every fight. All week long at supper I'd beg my mother to let me wear a regular St. Bridget's uniform. All week long she refused. All week long she'd threaten me with death if I didn't get my butt up for school on time. I cannot recall just how many fistfights I got into that first week, but I do remember the outcome of every one of them; none went in my favor.

Finally Dad talked to her and I was allowed to quit with the white knee socks and beanie. But now that I'd been marked as the joke of the neighborhood, it was easy for kids to pick on me.

I had two obvious problems that I could do absolutely nothing about. First, as the new kid in the neighborhood I was an easy target, a fact that is just part of growing up anyplace. The new kids always get picked on for a while. But I had some physical attributes that were not going to go away quickly. Not only did I have a thick brogue, but I stuttered when I spoke. Each and every time

31

Sister Mary Issacs, my first-grade teacher, would ask me a question in the classroom, I'd take minutes to stammer out an answer. The harder I tried the harder the laughter resounded. My face would get tight and hot. I could feel my ears burning and my eyes watering. I remember Sister Mary Issacs yelling at the class to be quiet and instantly the room would hush. I would stutter my answer and the entire room would begin in a fit of laughter all over again. Finally Sister Mary Issacs just gave up. After a while all the teachers stopped calling on me; it just was too much of a chore, and far too time-consuming to wait for an answer.

Recess never saved me. As soon as I hit the pavement the big kids would begin in with quacking sounds, making fun of my duck feet. I was a skinny little kid and to this day both my feet point outward at a forty-five-degree angle. In fact, I still laugh today when I see pictures of myself with the white knee socks and beanie. I looked like a bad-ass duck.

Everything came to a head when I was ten, a year after I first began school at St. Bridget's. For that first year I'd deliberately removed myself from a good portion of trouble. I had stopped reacting to being teased and was considered a quiet kid. I found a way to become invisible to most in order to avoid trouble. A couple of things helped me along the way, of course. First, I wasn't the new kid anymore. Somebody else would always come along, someone with big ears or a hooked nose, and most of the recess bullies would ignore me in favor of new prey. But it was Grumpy Grondin — and a mundane nickname — that completely altered the course of my life.

Grumpy was the neighborhood bully. He lived on Second Street almost directly behind our house. I can't recall one distinguishing characteristic about him. He didn't have red hair; he wasn't big and he wasn't too small. Grumpy just picked on everybody and anybody who he assumed would be scared of him and wouldn't fight back. Grumpy called me Donkey. He'd parade around me at recess making deep, guttural sounds like a donkey's that would draw the whole schoolyard's attention. I'd be so embarrassed that I wanted to run home and hide. In bed at night, alone in the dark, right before I'd fall off to sleep I would think of ways to end my shame. Grumpy's antics were so humiliating. He made me feel as if something about me was fundamentally wrong or flawed, that I was truly different from all the other kids.

Every moment I was at St. Bridget's, whether at recess or in the corridors, I made a conscious effort to be aware of Grumpy's presence. I figured that as long as I didn't see him in front of me, I was safe. When I did see him I'd work hard at removing myself from his radar. But on those days that I failed to avoid him, the embarrassment would haunt me all day and through the night for weeks.

I can still vividly recall the exact moment I decided to end the embarrassment once and for all. Grumpy had spotted me on the playground after lunch. I had just begun a conversation with a new student and thought for sure we'd become great friends. But without warning Grumpy decided to do his donkey routine. This time it seemed to linger forever. The pain in my chest was like rubbing alcohol on an open wound. At first I focused on the new boy's blue eyes. I figured if we could just hold each other's stare Grumpy would go away. But when the little boy's eyes started to smile, it was all over. Before I knew it he started to laugh and joined in making donkey sounds with all the others.

That night, after everybody in the house went to sleep, I began my quest for revenge. My history of street fighting was mostly pathetic. I wasn't dumb — I knew I couldn't stop Grumpy with my fists. And I knew if I tried he'd destroy me. I'd sink deeper into fear. But most of all I'd become the object of even more ridicule.

It was Ma's western movies that ultimately saved me. I knew from watching them that the guy who was quickest to draw his weapon always won; the biggest and strongest guys seemed to always get gunned down in the middle of the street. The cowboys who hid comfortably behind the largest rocks ambushed and destroyed the Indians every time.

My dad had no guns in our house, but that night in the darkness my mind went to work on the perfect substitute. Under my brother's bed I found the bow and arrow my mother had given me the previous Christmas. I tiptoed across the hall to the kitchen. The darkness turned to pearly gray where the moon's light entered the kitchen windows. I couldn't afford to turn a light on. Slowly I opened the drawer that held Ma's kitchen knives. I found the sharpest one right on top. Back in my room, I picked up the arrow and snapped the wood at the tip, right over the rubber arrowhead. It was a perfect break. Now all I had to do was whittle a nice sharp point and return Ma's kitchen knife without being caught. Because there would be no way to explain it, no way to fast talk or lie. The point of my new arrow was so sharp, anyone who found it could come to no other conclusion but that there was malevolent intent.

Early the next morning I wrapped the bow and arrow securely in an old pillowcase, tucked it up under my jacket, and headed for school. Ma was in the kitchen cleaning the morning dishes. I squeezed the pillowcase under my elbow, said goodbye, and left about fifteen minutes early. It was the first time I remembered the bubbling swell of butterflies in my stomach and the satisfying taste of revenge in the back of my throat.

I found a great hiding spot on the corner immediately before St. Bridget's, in an alley that separated our stickball lot from a tenement. It was a perfect spot, both for hiding my weapon and for the assault itself. A wooden fence with one-inch slats blocked off the alley. Stairs led to the cellars below ground. I recall carefully placing the pillowcase on a small ledge of an inside wall and covering it with some loose rocks. Then I went off to school as usual.

Every time Grumpy Grondin walked by me in the corridors at school that day I just grinned. I wasn't scared of him anymore.

Nothing was going to stop me from getting even. I'd made up my mind. Never once did the thought of not following through with my plan come into my head. I just knew that it was the right thing to do. It makes no difference if you're young or old; justice always brings a sense of confidence. Besides, it was the only way to stop being a donkey. I couldn't wait for the after-school bell to ring.

The rush of adrenaline when I heard the bell gave me such a sense of competence. I felt alive. My feet hit the floor running. I flung the rear door to St. Bridget's open, and I was down the stairs and in the alley in a flash. I found the pillowcase, located the arrow, and sat down on the top step waiting, my bow in place. My heart was racing but I wasn't afraid. I was focused, I was set, and I was ready to act. Minutes felt like hours as I watched several kids passing the alley from school through the thin slats in the fence. I felt as if I was in a sound tunnel. No outside noises could penetrate. I was invisible.

The first sound to break my concentration was Grumpy's obnoxious voice. It seemed to hover in the air even before I saw him. Hugging the ground, I crept slowly to the edge of the fence. I made sure the end of my arrow was firmly set into the bow. And then, through a one-inch opening, I saw him, surrounded by his friends.

I jumped up and readied my arrow all in one motion. In a heartbeat his arrogant grin deserted him. He froze. He couldn't talk. I was standing two feet in front of him with a razor-sharp arrow pointing directly between his eyeballs.

Everything went to slow motion and sound seemed to evaporate. I took a deep breath and drew the bowstring as far back as I could. Grumpy's mouth opened and his eyes grew to the size of golf balls. Snap. A sudden whoosh broke the silence as the bow released. Instantly the tip of the arrow found its mark and everything around me quickened. I'd shot Grumpy square in the forehead.

But the arrow didn't penetrate his skull. It just bounced off his hard head into the street. The silly bastard ran home crying, blood squirting everyplace. He sounded like my baby brother with a dirty diaper, wailing to be changed. He wasn't so tough anymore. It's funny how fast things change when you're that young. All the neighborhood kids were laughing at Grumpy now.

I picked up the arrow, broke it into several pieces, and threw it into the grassy field next to my house. I wasn't really worried about anybody finding the evidence. Somehow I knew disposing of it wouldn't be the end of the story. I was one hundred percent sure that I'd be in a lot of trouble at home. But at that moment, flush with a feeling of the new power I'd achieved, those were consequences that I could live with.

Everything was fine until Dad got home. Ma was in the kitchen getting supper when I heard the first knock at the front door. It was Grumpy Grondin's father. My dad, being a gentleman, invited him into the kitchen for tea. I was at the end of the hallway, right inside my bedroom door, listening to the tale of Grumpy's head being cut open with a bow and arrow.

"Paddy," Dad yelled.

I swallowed hard but was confident. I'd expected all along to be caught and I wasn't scared when I entered the kitchen. Dad looked more confused than angry. I remember taking a quick peek at Mom by the stove. Her eyes didn't hold fire. Right then I knew I'd have a chance to show that I'd had no other choice — that I'd acted in my own self-defense.

"Did you shoot an arrow at Mr. Grondin's son after school today?" Dad asked.

I didn't hesitate. "Yes!"

"Why did you do that, Paddy?" Dad seemed impatient. Ma just listened. She never stepped on my dad's place in our family

"He makes fun of me all day at school. He calls me Donkey and pushes me around at recess. I couldn't stop him. So I shot him in the head with my bow and arrow."

"You could have taken his eye out," Grumpy's father jumped in.

"But he just won't leave me alone. I just want to be left alone. I never bother him."

Dad sent me to my room and ordered me to shut the door tight. I tried hard to hear what was being said in the kitchen, but it was all mumbling. I could only make out a word here and there. It must have been a good fifteen minutes before they called me back into the kitchen. Nobody had moved. Dad had finished his tea and the teabag rested on top of his spoon.

"You have to fight him, Paddy," my father instructed. "Get your shoes on. We're going to Grondin's backyard right now. This will finish it."

I never hesitated. I got my shoes and followed Dad out the front door. Ma winked at me. Every step I took as I followed Dad down Court Lane brought me courage. Something came over me that day that stayed with me through Vietnam, through the Southie gang war, and inside prison. I saw something in Grumpy's eyes that has given me the edge in every conflict I've been involved in since: I saw fear.

The fight didn't last long. At first we pushed and shoved. I got him on the ground. We wrestled and swung wild. But he was no match for me; his heart just wasn't in it. Every time I looked into his eyes I knew that he still saw that arrow heading toward his forehead. Grumpy quit and fear controlled him from that moment on. He never called me Donkey again.

Back then, as I watched westerns with Ma in our living room, I was too young to understand what I know to be true today. It wasn't God that made men equal. It was a weapon.

4. THE MULLEN GANG

It wasn't easy being Irish in America back in the 1950s: there were no handouts or food-stamp programs, just families making sure everybody had enough to get by. But the day I joined the Mullen gang, everything changed. We were the gang of enterprising thieves. If you were a Mullen you always had money in your pocket, and some to spread to your family, too.

But let me correct two perceptions right now. First, I want to start with the truth about South Boston residents: most people in Southie weren't criminals. The majority of South Boston's residents were proud citizens just like my mom and dad. They worked hard every day just to pay some of the bills and put food on the table, and they dreamed of giving their children a better start in life than they had. But media and myth have created a stereotype of South Boston for all those who live on the other side of the bridges. Believe me when I tell you that we, the residents, do not live in a place that even remotely resembles the stereotype. The media turned us into white monsters who hated black children. Everyplace I'd go back in the 1970s, the moment I'd say "I'm from Southie" people would automatically paint me as a racist. All they saw on the evening news were images of armed militia on our rooftops and angry white people fighting outside of South Boston High as black children were escorted off yellow school buses. Forced busing stole our neighborhoods. We just wanted to hang on to them. They were our schools, directly across the street from our houses, and they were stolen from us. We had no choice but to fight — to lose our neighborhoods was unfathomable and inexcusable. But nobody in the media showed the truth about our struggle.

The other myth I want to dispel is the myth of James J. "Whitey" Bulger. Whitey fooled people in South Boston into believing he was Robin Hood while he made a pact with FBI agent John Connolly and gave away all his friends. The truth about Jimmy Bulger is he is a rat, a pedophile, a rapist, and a sociopath who was dishonorably discharged from the U.S. Air Force. And he is the man directly responsible for bringing drugs into South Boston. It was Jimmy Bulger who lined his pockets with drug dealers' protection money as young boys from the Old Colony Housing Project overdosed on heroin and lay in wake at Jakie O'Brien's Funeral Home on Broadway.

Ironically, every day Jimmy Bulger remains at large his self-created myth grows. For ten years now he's been on the FBI's Most Wanted list; he was number one on that list until Bin Laden knocked him to second position after 9/11. Many people in Southie were afraid of Whitey.

I don't want to sound self-righteous here, because I was a criminal also. I stole for food, I stole to pay the bills, I stole to support the IRA, and I stole to provide hope for my three children. In fact, I'm certain I was born to be a criminal. It's the one talent God gave me that I capitalized on. As far back in my memory as I can go, one thing I know for certain — trouble has a way of finding me. Today I understand: I am a born criminal, and criminals attract trouble.

I'm not ashamed about being a criminal, because I was damn good at what I did. But being a Mullen made you a different kind of criminal. None of the Mullens were fakes; we wouldn't conceive of giving up a friend for personal gain. Honor, trust, and courage were qualities I learned as a teenager inside the Mullen gang. Besides, my dad always said we couldn't have moved into a better South Boston neighborhood. "It's a perfect fit for young Pat," he said. "We moved right into a pack of thieves."

In the early sixties, gangs in Southie were like cows in Vermont

— every corner had them. But the Saints, the Mullens, and the Killeëns were the gangs that everybody spoke of. The Saints were from D Street on the lower West Side; the Saints were tough but they couldn't match our strength man for man. The Killeens were organized criminals who controlled all the gambling and book-making in South Boston. Everybody paid them tribute. Me? I was a Mullen. The Mullen gang had been around since the early fifties; the gang took its name from a square in South Boston where we hung out that was named after a World War I veteran, James Joseph Mullen. But we weren't organized criminals; we were wharf rats and were highly respected as thieves. Our expertise came in our ability to hijack trucks from the wharf. We mastered the art of "tailgating" off trucks loading and unloading at the warehouses by the waterfront. We'd run a little diversion in front of the truck while two or three of us grabbed boxes of cigarettes or cases of tuna and crabmeat off the tailgate. Who could catch us?

As a teenager I hung out with Louie Lentini and Jerry Shea in the old Lighthouse Tavern down on East Third Street. Every night the place was packed full of longshoremen and thieves. In the summer they had a nice area out back with tables and a bar-becue. It was fascinating to be inside the Lighthouse Tavern shining shoes and watching the thieves make deals and counting their money. It looked so easy and exciting. I think I was only four-teen or fifteen when I realized my ambition in life was to become a thief.

During the days most of the Mullens hung around at Al's Spa, across the street from the Massachusetts Bay Transportation Authority (MBTA) car barn, where the old electric trolley cars would come in to turn around. Al had booths set up inside and would sell beer and whiskey illegally. Nobody cared about liquor licenses back then — even off-duty cops drank at Al's. It was a neighborhood thing; it was just accepted.

On those scorching summer days we'd watch freight ships the size of football fields being maneuvered by tugboats into the channel as we cooled off in Boston Harbor. On our side of the waterway stood wooden platforms that rose forty feet into the air. Cranes rested on the platforms and dumped coal from the ships, forming black mountains. I can still see Jackie Nee, one of the older Mullens (and no relation to me), gracefully climbing to the top of the coal heap and leaping headfirst in a perfect swan dive, plunging deep into the midnight-blue waters.

There was lots to do in South Boston, the best place in America for an Irish kid to grow up. We Mullens always found ways to keep ourselves occupied, sometimes legitimately. Each morning we drank fresh milk and ate donuts stolen from the corner variety. After breakfast five or six of us would grab the Mullens' small red Radio Flyer wagon and load redeemable bottles discarded in the neighborhood bushes. By afternoon we'd hit the package store, cash in the bottles, and divide up the money. I don't remember how much we made at the end of the day but it was enough to get us to return on a daily basis. Every Sunday a guy would show up in a station wagon and load papers into our Radio Flyer. We pulled that wagon up and down Castle Island until there were no papers left. I remember one summer we even sold ice cream on Castle Island for a commission.

Actually, there was no good reason for a Mullen to be broke in South Boston.

But no doubt the best part of being a Mullen was the location of our home turf. Southie is a peninsula, with streets numbered First through Ninth running east to west. Back then First Street was the only way out of Castle Island. Every truck that left the docks had to go through our neighborhood. That meant that each ship's cargo had to pass through our streets to reach its final destination.

One of the Mullens' favorite grabs was pig tin, a type of lead that came in blocks. It was precious metal back then. The ships brought tons of blocks onto our docks. Each block was worth eighty or ninety bucks, but you could only grab a few at a time without getting caught.

Louie, Paulie, and I would watch from the bushes across the street as the longshoreman would load blocks of pig tin into the open-bed trucks. Once the pig tin was visible above the top of the truck, they'd cover the blocks with canvas and tie them down tight with nylon rope.

We'd get the go-ahead just before the trucks rolled. The older Mullens would watch for the driver to climb into the cab and then give us a whistle. Louie and I would break hard for the rear of the truck, trying desperately not to be spotted. If we made it without anybody yelling at us, we'd crawl under the canvas and ride up First Street, pushing blocks off the back of the truck the whole way. The older guys would follow the trucks in cars, collecting the pig tin, all the way to the lights. As soon as the truck hit L Street we'd hop down and jump into the waiting cars. A dozen blocks of pig tin was considered a good grab, and the driver never knew the difference.

My mother hated the Mullens. She knew we were up to no good. I'll never forget the time we were all drinking beer around the vacant buildings off Third Street. I was fifteen. It had to be two or three o'clock in the morning. It was a Friday night, a hot summer night with no breeze; I think Louie was the first to see my mother coming. From where I was sitting I could see only her silhouette as she moved quickly into the moonlight. Her slippers scuffled on the cobblestone as she came closer. Some of the younger guys ran. I hid behind the wall, inside some bushes. At the sight of her marching implacably forward, her hair up in a bun and her thin summer nightgown pressed closely against her, I knew I was in deep trouble if she caught me.

"Mrs. Nee is coming." Whispers bounced around the shadows.

"Patrick Nee, get your ass here quick," she said, her brogue cutting through the darkness.

I wouldn't come out at first, but the older guys wanted her gone and pushed me forward. She would rummage through every bush until she found me anyway. She'd twist my ear and drag me past the gang, all sitting there frozen stiff.

"Ma, you're embarrassing me," I spoke softly.

"You should all be ashamed of yourselves," she yelled, as though she wanted everybody in a two-block radius to hear. "Down here with all these gunslingers, thieves, and drunks."

"Good evening Mrs. Nee," McNally, one of the older guys blurted out.

"James McNally don't give me that 'good evening' crap. Go home to your wife and kids. And I see you over there hiding like a dog, Tommy Sullivan. Get back home this instant or I'll tell your mother where I saw ya."

Nobody ever talked back to her — my mother was nobody to cross.

One of the hardest things to hide from my mother were the fist-fights. I got my ass kicked in most of them, but fighting with the Mullens always improved my odds. We hardly ever lost a good fight. And each gang had a kid or two you didn't want to fight on your own.

One night we were scheduled to fight the Saints at the M Street Park. Word was out for all of us to show up in numbers. The Saints had numbers, too; most were rugged kids from the projects who wouldn't back down. Gerry Shea, Louie Lentini, and I got there around 10 P.M., probably an hour before the fight was set to start. We had a good thirty guys there, ranging in age from four-teen to twenty-one. One of the older guys was in charge of strategy. He split us up — half of us hid behind the wall and the other half waited in plain view. Those of us who were hiding were to charge once the Saints and our boys met face to face.

But only one car of Saints showed. Red O'Brien, Joe L, a kid named McGrail, and a driver I didn't know got out and walked into the center of the park. We thought it was a trap. Most of us froze, waiting for a line of cars to come screeching up behind us. But nobody came to help them. They had balls, so we gave them a fair fight. The Mullens picked four guys and they fought, but nobody was into it. Nobody really won. It just ended — Red and his boys drove away, and the Mullens went to the wall for beers. How could you not respect those Saints after that?

It's always fun to kick somebody's ass when you don't start the fight. One day toward the end of the summer of 1961, bored with swimming, a group of us was sitting up on Castle Hill under the shade of the maple trees sipping some cold beers. The hill on Castle Island was the best place to be on a hot day. We could watch the girls in their bikinis, cool off in the water, or sit up on the highest tree overlooking South Boston Harbor. And the location, fifty yards from the white sands of the public beach, was elevated enough to make it a secure getaway if need be.

I think it was Bo MacIntyre who spotted the "outsiders" watching us from the edge of the water, right next to the parking lot. We were outnumbered maybe two to one, but we had no choice but to challenge them. Castle Island was our neighborhood, and if they wanted to call us on it, the Mullens weren't about to run.

Of course, anyone who wasn't from Southie was considered an "outsider." But these kids from the Majestics gang from Roxbury stood out like sore thumbs. Some were all black or brown but the majority of them were white. And right or wrong, the color of the minority provoked immediate tension and unease anywhere in South Boston. As soon as they spotted us staring down at them, their leader, a muscular kid in white gym shorts, led the charge.

He was stupid. His first mistake was attacking us going up a hill. You should never attack going up a hill. We had an insurmountable advantage. Their second mistake: they never calculated what we were doing on that hill and how that would affect the outcome of the fight.

"Charge them!" somebody yelled. "Take a full bottle of beer in each hand and charge them."

The momentum was ours. Crack. We ran right through them. I remember the sudden thud and a dull "whoosh" as beer bottles exploded on skulls. I saw two or three of them rolling back toward the beach. Others ran for the water, as if it would protect them. I saw a young mother holding her infant, an old lady screaming, and others just taking in the action. It was South Boston. What else were they going to do?

I never felt the pipe hit the back of my head or the knife puncture my arm. My adrenalin was gushing and I only saw their wounded — their young black leader, his face booted into fresh raw hamburger like you'd see at the butcher. We left him there and headed for the shoreline to finish off those who had retreated. They were scared and defeated, and the taste of victory coursed through me. The massacre lasted a solid half hour. Most of them were down on the beach or hiding among the onlookers. I saw some of them swimming out to the raft at the same time that I heard the police sirens.

Again, we were in the driver's seat. Castle Island was our playground. We hopped over the chain link fence that separated the beach from the docks. By the time the Metropolitan District Commission police blocked off and closed down the island, we'd snuck out behind them.

I graduated to breaking and entering into warehouses outside the neighborhood when I was fifteen. Then when I was sixteen the older guys introduced us to handguns, and our criminal careers suddenly changed direction. We'd heard that the Teamster Shed at the South Boston shipyard paid the workers in cash every Tuesday. We watched from the shadows for several weeks, then hit them fast with masks — guns drawn — without incident.

By the time I turned seventeen the Mullens had become my second family. The bonds you establish as a thief are very similar to those of a family. Something happens to your insides when you stick a gun in somebody's face. It brings you to a place where fear does not exist — it simply resolves. At that instant you completely understand that your friends, standing in front of you or behind you, are counting on you — and you on them. No words need to be exchanged. It is a reality that cannot be explained unless you've lived it.

The day came when Gerry, Louie, and I knew we had to move on. We were seventeen and school was a waste of time. For my mother's sake I enrolled at Cathedral High School and was on the swim team. But the brothers at Cathedral asked me to leave; they told my parents I was disruptive. I tried a year at Southie High and played junior varsity football, but it was too hard to study when all I could think about was crime. There were far too many ways to make easy money. My parents had come to accept my thieving, and I made sure my brothers didn't get involved. My mother and father wanted that.

Bored with school, it didn't take me long to figure out what my next step would be. It was 1962. The United States Marine Corps sported a long list of members from the Mullen gang. I remember Gerry and me sitting for hours listening to the older Mullens telling war stories from World War II and Korea. Pete and Wally Mansfield were highly decorated combat Marines who'd been in the middle of hell during World War II. But Paulie Yanovich had seen the worst — I listened for hours on a hot August night as he wove his tale. It fascinated me; I couldn't wait until I was old enough to become a marine.

One night down by the wall Louie, Jerry, and I decided we'd go into the service together. My father had to sign the papers. Both he and my mother thought it was the best move for me. They thought it would straighten me out, teach me discipline.

On July 1, 1962, I became a United States citizen; I left for Parris Island, South Carolina, one week later. My recruiter told my parents not to worry. We weren't at war, so there was nothing to fear in me joining the Marines. On the day I left Southie, nobody would have thought that the United States would lose over fifty thousand men in Vietnam over the course of the next ten years.

5. THE STUTTERING MARINE

Nothing exceptional happened during basic training.
I did what every Marine recruit was expected to do: I survived twelve weeks of pure hell.

The recruiter wouldn't let us go down to Parris Island on the buddy system. Gerry, Louie, and I had to leave a week apart from one another. For no good reason I was chosen to go last. My mother cried a little. I was only seventeen and the first of her children to leave home. But her tears didn't last long — she knew it was best for me to leave Southie while I still could. My mother was an important figure in my life. Sure, I was always in a jam, but I never set out to cause her pain or worry. She was a strong woman, and she was my very first teacher. Her commitment to our family gave me my first lessons in determination and tenacity.

I gave my mother a hug, shook my father's hand, and said good-bye to my brothers and sisters. Twenty minutes later I was at South Station with a small suitcase, the voucher the recruiter had given me, and an envelope with pictures of my family to remind me of South Boston, waiting to board a train.

Outside the gates of Parris Island I was loaded onto a bus with other young kids I'd never seen before. I remember the exuberant smiles on the faces of the assistant drill instructors who barked out directions. I'd been warned by the older Mullens who'd been down there what to expect, but still, these guys were just having too much fun.

It had been an extremely hot July day and the humidity on the bus turned the world outside into a soupy, gray haze. "Put your head between your legs and kiss your ass good-bye," yelled the marine in charge of transportation.

Just before I did what he told me, I looked up and saw gates with a sign that read ENTERING PARRIS ISLAND. There was no way off the island except one narrow road, and we were on it. The barracks and training facilities were a mile in and were completely surrounded by mosquito-filled swamps. I'd heard about guys trying to escape because they couldn't take it anymore — I'm sure the marines who were transporting us didn't want us to know the way out.

When the bus finally came to a stop I didn't want to lift my head off my lap to see where we were, so I rolled my face slightly to the right, just enough to catch a glimpse of the window across from me. I could see a bright area and hear the sound of boots meeting the pavement outside.

"Off the fucking bus you bunch of low-life, scum-sucking assholes."

"Now! Now! Not yesterday or tomorrow. Get the fuck out off those seats!"

"Oh look at this fat-ass turkey. He's definitely gonna get skull fucked by me."

"Shit, look at the fuckin' head on this stinkin' black chicken-shit donkey mother fucker. Guess the rest of his body must have run down his daddy's leg."

We just sat there paralyzed. Some guys buried their heads deeper up their asses just trying to hide.

"Go! This is fuckin' America, asswipes. Don't you understand American? Get the fuck off the bus now or you'll run till your dicks fall off."

Seat by seat we started to file out. A part of me wanted to smile, but I knew if I did I'd be fucked. I think it was just nerves. It reminded me of the way I'd feel before entering the front door of my home in Southie after the nuns had sent me home for something I'd done wrong.

"What are you fuckin' looking at homo boy?" An enormous

black marine with a scar over his right eye screamed at a wimpy kid wearing thick black glasses several feet in front of me.

"Nothing," his voice cracked.

"Do you like me, queer-boy?"

"No sir," he replied.

"You wanna kiss me, faggot?"

"No, no, sir."

"You think I'm fuckin' pretty? Where you from, homo?"

"Houston sir."

"Houston? Are there a lot of faggots who suck dick in Houston?"

The kid behind me was blowing air out his nose in a feeble attempt to keep from laughing. I bit down extremely hard on the inside of my mouth. It hurt, but even at seventeen I knew gum pain was better than what this gorilla could do to me if I slipped up and let him know just how funny he was.

The kid didn't answer. I couldn't see but he might have been crying. I thought his shoulders seemed to be trembling, but I didn't want to appear too inquisitive.

"Don't look at the drill instructor unless you're told to look at one of us. Get your sweaty faggot asses off this bus and line up as a platoon," screamed a white drill instructor who had just stepped onto the bus.

It wasn't funny anymore. The smell of fear filled my nostrils. I could almost hear the sounds of the somersaults inside my gut. Fear smells just like rancid chicken soup, and I hate chicken soup. But puking wasn't an option.

Outside, away from the claustrophobic confines of the bus, I got the immediate sense that nobody could prepare us for what was to come. For sure this place wasn't South Boston. But for twelve weeks I could survive anything. I mean, they couldn't kill us.

Light shining down from the poles strategically placed around the buildings cut the darkness into beams made up of tiny particles of moisture that seemed to obliterate all color. Everything looked black and white. I remember sprinting, trying desperately to stay close to the kid in front of me. It was midnight, everybody was frightened, we were all stupid kids, and nobody knew what to do next.

"Fall in, you queer bastards. Find two yellow foot marks that go together and fall in."

"What are you? A fucking retard, son?"

It was hard to tell who was yelling, there were so many of them, and after the incident with the kid wearing glasses I wasn't about to make eye contact with anybody in uniform. Some kid around 5'5" and wearing a gray sweat-stained t-shirt had found the only way to not line up properly.

"Look what we got here. A fucking retarded queer. Now here is a boy who don't take it up the ass because he don't know where his ass is. Well, queer-boy, we spent all day yesterday hand-painting those feet. We even made them yellow and retard proof. But of course one of you cocksucking queers has two right legs. Get to the back of the line and find your feet, Scumbag."

It was all a shock. I remember lying on the top bunk my first night. I'd left a paradise in South Boston, being part of a gang that owned the streets and from a neighborhood where I could go and come as I pleased to a mighty fist right up the ass here at Parris Island. I was scared. But I was a Mullen. There was no way in hell I contemplated quitting even for a second.

Besides, I really figured the bus incident was just a first-night experience — I thought for sure the drill instructors only had to live up to their reputation. But I was wrong.

"Drop your cocks and grab your socks!" A voice crashed into my sleep.

It was still dark when we hit the yellow foot markers outside our barracks. The cool air made my sweat bite cold against my back. Before we had a chance to think, prepare, or look sideways, we were running full-ass-out, following the enormous drill sergeant up a hill. We ran and ran until death seemed like the better option.

Staff Sergeant Kemp was the senior drill instructor. He looked to be about forty and he wore a short-sleeved shirt that cut tightly into the lower part of his biceps. He was from Georgia, the deep South. I remember his drawl, how each syllable hung and seemed to penetrate deeper into your eardrum. It wasn't long before Kemp was to dramatically influence my Marine Corps experience.

We'd just gotten into formation after chow. "Nee, front and center," he screeched.

"Sss sir, yyes sir." I couldn't help it, the stammer just happened.

"You're one of those queer Yankee boys from South Boston."

"Sir, the reeecruuit is from South Boston," I replied.

"We got ourselves a real live stuttering Yankee faggot."

"Sir, the recruit stutters sir."

"You cannot stststuttter and be a fuckin' marine, you queer, stuttering Yankee piece of whale shit."

"Sir, the recruit will try not to stststutter."

"Try? Turds try. Marines do. Turn around, remove your guidebook, and proceed to read. Loud and clear Yankee faggot. If you fuckin' stststutter once, drop down and give me twenty-five push-ups."

Soon it got to be daily procedure. There I was out in front of my company, reading the guidebook, stuttering, and pumping out push-ups. But it didn't bother me. A Southie mentality was deeply implanted inside, and nobody could take that from me. The drill instructors soon recognized my indifference to what other people thought of my stuttering. I became the right guide, which was a meritorious promotion. All the right guides were hand picked by the drill instructors. It didn't mean that you were better than the other recruits, it just meant that you were one of the recruits that stood out throughout the physical activities of the day.

As right guide I led my company every place we went on Parris Island. My job was to march outside the column holding up a six-foot wooden staff with our platoon's red flag on top. We were platoon 350 and over the flag was a silver guide that screwed onto the staff. It looked like a spear resting on the staff's tip. It was my job to always keep the guide nice and shiny and to protect the chow line. When you're right guide you never let anybody except a marine who has graduated from basic training cut in front of you in the chow line. As right guide you cannot let any other recruit that isn't in your platoon step in front of your guys.

One day we'd marched to chow and I'd placed our flag in the appropriate position out in the front of the hall, unscrewed the guide, and stuck it in my pocket so nobody would steal it. Out of nowhere I heard some commotion. I turned to see a huge recruit, about 6'5" and 230 pounds, making his way around my platoon. I had no choice but to confront him. It was my job. It was my platoon.

I stepped into his way. "End of the line," I said. "You ain't cuttin' in front of our platoon."

He stopped inches from my chest, and I could see him thinking about his options. I was 5'9" and 165 pounds, so I'm sure he wasn't thinking that hard. My neck was fully extended just trying to stare into his eyes.

"I'll see you outside after chow," he said, backing up.

"Fucking right you will," I nodded, thinking it wouldn't go anywhere in a controlled environment like Parris Island. Naturally I'd just do the same thing I'd do any other day: fill my plate, sit with my platoon, and wait for the drill instructors to give us the okay to eat. But the moment I started to chew my food things somehow didn't seem right. Usually the drill instructors would be pressing their faces close, screaming shit to make you laugh, just fucking with your head. Nobody bothered our platoon today. It was quiet until I saw the recruits across from me stop eating and look behind me. Instantly, I felt this big ham hock of a hand pinching my left shoulder.

"You ready to go outside, boy?" It was him. I didn't even have to turn.

"Yeah, let's go."

What more could I say? It was a test of my resolve. Everybody inside my platoon and all the drill instructors were waiting to see if I'd stand up to this giant who couldn't even wait until I finished my chow to kick my ass. There went my belief — or better stated, my hope — that the fight wouldn't materialize. The drill instructors didn't miss a trick: they'd seen him cut in line, and they'd seen him offer me out after chow. They could have stopped it.

As soon as we left the mess hall we double-timed into the woods; a recruit never just walked anywhere on Parris Island. The other guy was a step or two in front of me. That was part of my strategy. No way was he faster than me. If I let him get behind me I wouldn't have a chance to see his first move. But I knew that my time was about to run out. I had to improve my odds. I had to come up with something fast.

My eyes were focused on his feet and hips. I saw his feet grip as his hips started to turn. Bang. I unloaded four or five shots to the side of his head, right in the soft spot of the temple. I felt the sudden vibration of each hit, starting from his skull and running down my elbows all the way to my jawline. He just looked at me and smiled. To this day I don't know if he even knew that I hit him. From that moment on I was glad we were in the woods. It would have been worse for my platoon to watch me get pummeled.

Things went from bad to terrible very, very quickly. He finally wrestled me to the ground, sat on my chest, and drove his knees into each of my biceps. I couldn't move, he was just too heavy.

Boom. Boom. Boom. He had me locked to the ground and was

punching me in the face. It was all happening too fast for panic. I couldn't feel the impact at first, but the shot to the nose filled my eyes with water. I couldn't see. Everything began to spin. It felt like a ten-inch nail had been driven behind my eyes. Bitter, warm blood filled my mouth and dripped slowly down the back of my throat.

"You quit, boy?" he asked with a humorous stare.

I spit in his face. The only thing I had left was my blood.

"Fuck you," I managed.

I wouldn't quit. Finally he stopped; he just got tired of hitting me. He picked me up and pushed me toward the blacktop just as his platoon was coming by. I saw the drill instructor evaluate our situation, then move his eyes quickly away and pretend we weren't there. "Look at him," the drill instructor yelled, "this good old boy just doesn't have an ounce of quit in him."

I ran back to my barracks as fast as I could. We were in 350, the third deck of the brick building. My next test would be getting past my drill instructor. Since fighting was prohibited I had to sneak in to the barracks. My chest and the front of my pants, right above the knees, were saturated in my blood. But as soon as I came through the front hatch it was over.

"Nee, front and center."

I ran up to Sergeant Younger and jumped to attention. Younger was writing something the entire time he was looking me up and down. He wasn't a big man — he was about my size — and when he talked his eyes squinted almost shut, like he was trying to conceal a grin.

"You fighting, boy?"

"No sir."

"Don't lie to me boy. Were you fighting?"

"Sir, the recruit was not fighting," I replied. If I'd told the truth I would have been disciplined.

He paused.

"You're full of shit, recruit. Did you win or lose?"

"Sir, the recruit was not fighting."

"Don't look like you did too good, Nee. Hit the shower."

From that moment on I was looked upon differently. I'd fought a guy twice my size. Got my ass handed to me. I shut up. Denied it. And that made me victorious in the eyes of the rest of my platoon. No way was I going to back down or quit. I learned never to quit growing up in Southie.

I was one of seven guys promoted at graduation. I'll never forget the morning I marched with my platoon onto the parade grounds at Parris Island. My uniform was new, tailored for me, dry cleaned and pressed. My hat sat perfectly over my forehead. The tie wedged close to my neck. I had my private first class strip sewn on the left shoulder of my uniform and my marksman badge sewn to the front of my shirt. The ceremony gave me the chills and the muscles in my jaw became rigid. I was proud to be a United States Marine.

All the graduates stood at attention as the day's ceremony marched on. Any memory of the physical and mental anguish of the last twelve weeks was erased by the orange and gold Marine Corps flag that flew proud against the blue sky. I watched my friends' parents listening to a Marine Corps general speaking of our goals. My parents didn't have the money to make the trip for my graduation. I wished they were there when Sergeant Younger spoke to me after graduation.

"Don't call me 'sir' anymore, Nee. You're a United States Marine. Now you're expected to carry on the tradition."

I'll never in my life forget the sense of honor, pride, and accomplishment that swelled in my being when Younger shook my hand. South Boston and the Mullens gave me an excellent foundation for my life, but the drill instructors of Parris Island instilled in me a confidence that has never died.

6. HAWAII

Vietnam saved me from the brig. It saved me from being disgraced, court-martialed, and sent back to Southie with a dishonorable discharge. Ironically, it was what I'd learned in South Boston — standing up for what I believe — that almost brought me to disgrace.

In the fall of 1963 I returned from a Mediterranean cruise with the 6th Marine Brigade. It was right before President Kennedy was assassinated. My company was stationed at Camp Lejeune, North Carolina, and I hated every minute of my time in that place. I had no real reason for such disdain except that it wasn't Southie. It was just a hot, slimy place to be, both in temperature and appearance. The nearest town was Jacksonville, North Carolina, and it was brimming with honky tonk bars, pawn shops, hookers, and tattoo parlors. Every time we got leave, the marines from the north would pool their money and drive as far away from that dump as we could.

It didn't take any persuading for me to move on when I saw an opportunity. I remember the air dripping with humidity. Most of us were bored as hell just waiting for something to happen. I'll never forget sitting in mess hall with a few grunts when the announcement was read. Most days, I was too busy eating to pay attention, but something about the smell of the moist air that day forced me to focus more than usual. Maybe I was beginning to get accustomed to the Marine Corps life, or maybe it was just what was supposed to happen. Fate had been taking care of me up to that point and I'm sure it grabbed my attention that day.

"Listen up," hollered an old-timer. "The 1st Marine Brigade in

Hawaii is looking for volunteers. Anyone interested report to the first sergeant immediately."

My legs hit the floor the same time the last syllable left his lips. I never looked back to see if anybody was following me. It didn't matter. I was determined to get out of North Carolina. It may sound funny to some people, but when you're raised in a place like South Boston it gets really hard to find a place that makes you as comfortable.

The first sergeant's office was behind the mess hall. The door was wide open, so I stepped through and watched for a few seconds while the sergeant read over papers on a brown clipboard.

I knocked. He didn't even look up. He just kept checking off pages with a pencil.

"Nee, is that you?"

"Yes," I responded, "but how did you know it was me?"

"Just a hunch you'd be the first to volunteer for this one. It's a perfect fit for you. We all know how much you like this duty station."

They did the paperwork. All I had to do was go home to South Boston for thirty days. That alone was worth volunteering. I reported back to Camp Pendleton in California the day after New Year's, 1964. Kennedy had just been laid to rest and most Americans were concerned about the future. The Irish loved Kennedy. JFK was one of ours. I waited at Pendleton for two weeks while volunteers arrived from all over the country. Soon we were bused to San Diego, where we boarded transport ships for Hawaii.

The ship was monstrous, and it didn't take a college education to get lost and not be missed. A few of us marines hooked up with some navy guys who showed us the ropes. We did absolutely nothing for two weeks and never got questioned. I didn't feel bad at all when I heard that most of the guys were scrubbing decks in the tropical sun. They may have been marines, but they weren't resourceful.

I assume we shipped into Pearl Harbor, but I cannot recall the exact details. I do remember being loaded in transport vehicles and trucked to Kaneohe Bay, on the windward side of Oahu, where the 1st Marine Brigade had set up their headquarters. It was a breathtaking base. The emerald green mountains held your back while the steel-blue Pacific woke you up in the early morning.

The very first morning on the island was the day we'd find out what we'd actually gotten ourselves into. We were standing in formation as the morning sun seemed to rise right out of the ocean. Personally I didn't give a damn what I'd be doing, because anything was better than where I'd been. But somehow when I saw the first sergeant coming out, I knew my luck was about to pay off one more time.

"Any recoilless riflemen here?" barked the first sergeant.

The Marine Corps trained us to react — I learned that if I stopped to think it would be too late. So I reacted. My hand went toward the sky with full confidence and an understanding that I had no idea what a recoilless rifle was or even exactly what it looked like. I might not have been a recoilless rifleman at the time, but I was about to become one.

No, I was not yet a recoilless rifleman. I was a grunt, and grunts humped every place they went. Humping is exactly what the word implies. A grunt walked in heat. A grunt walked in the rain. And you walked with sixty pounds strapped to your back. At Camp Lejeune we'd be out in the woods on maneuvers and just when it seemed you couldn't take another step, just when the sweat saturated your underwear, a "mule" — a flatbed truck with a 106 recoilless rifle sitting on the back — would drive by with two very happy marines with broad smiles resting quite comfortably next to the gun. I didn't care that I knew zilch about firing a 106. For the chance to ride on the tail end of a flatbed truck and watch Marines hump, I'd learn. It never crossed my mind that somebody might find out I was bluffing.

They took me at face value and sent me to the 3rd Battalion, 4th Marines 106S squad just next door. I started as an assistant gunner and six months later I became the best 106 gunner on the entire island of Hawaii. It was all training. The Marine Corps gave us the best possible odds at becoming excellent at whatever weapons we were assigned.

The 106 weighed about 460 pounds and the barrel was probably six feet long. The weapon sat on a tripod attached to the back of the mule. The gunner sat on the right side of the 106 and would spot the target through a site at the end of the barrel. A .50 caliber spotting rifle with a four-round magazine rested perfectly flush on the 106. The .50 caliber fired a tracer round, an illuminated round that helped you adjust and destroy the target. It took three marines to operate a 106. The shells came in crates, and it was the driver's responsibility to make sure we had plenty ready at the rear of the mule. The shells weighted twenty-seven pounds each. We had phosphorous rounds that burned away anything that entered their paths and heat rounds that blew the shit out of everything. The assistant gunner would line up the round, load the shell, depress, turn, and lock it in tight. The gunner would find the target, fire the .50 caliber, and adjust the site by watching the tracer round burn as it headed to its target. There were two small wheels strategically placed in front of the gunner. One would move the barrel right or left. The other was for elevation.

I could hit a moving vehicle at three hundred to five hundred yards in the first shot. In fact, in target practice I'd be shooting at vehicles running left to right on a track and I could locate a round inside the front windshield, through the driver's window. By the time the .50 caliber hits the enemy it's too late for him even to look up, because a 106 round is coming right up behind it.

We had our own 106 range at Kaneohe Bay with monthly and

sometimes bimonthly competitions. I think there would be four or five teams in line and we'd have to hit targets or moving vehicles on tracks. But it wasn't only accuracy that counted — it was speed. Speed always matters when your enemy is advancing. Winning entitled you to extra liberty; the victors got to leave the base on Friday morning, which meant an extra day at the beach. In Hawaii you couldn't go wrong with free time. The winners would be rested and ready to go out drinking while the other marines would just be getting off and heading into town. I won every time.

Most of us, marines and navy men, lived in bungalows off Waikiki Beach. They were small and sat close together, but the bungalows gave us a great place to go on weekends away from the base, away from everything but drinking, the beach, and women. The only problem was that sometimes the partying got out of hand, and in close quarters that can cause a disturbance.

One night a half dozen of us had come back from a bar downtown and decided to keep the party going. I guess we were playing the music a little loud. When you're a few sheets to the wind you pay no attention to how loud you are. Besides, we were marines — we worked hard all week and we played hard on weekends.

To this day I think the navy chief should have minded his own business. Out of nowhere he busts through our door without even knocking. I guess he thought we gave a rat's ass about his rank. He lived in the next bungalow, but I'd never seen him until that moment.

"Okay, the noise is over for this evening," he said. "It's time to turn the music off and get some sleep."

"Fuck off," somebody muttered.

"That is an order, marines!" the NCO snapped.

"What's the matter, sir?" I asked respectfully.

"Time for bed, asshole," he responded, without making eye contact.

That was a big mistake. He never should have said that to me, especially when I'm full of all kinds of alcohol.

"Just go back to where you came from," my friend Johnny Kaiser yelled at the navy chief, as he saw my face turn beet red.

I put the beer mug down real slow and deliberate. The navy man was no dummy; he'd seen resolve in a man's eyes before. Common sense told him to backpedal.

If I had it to do over again I would have let him leave. After all, we'd won. He would have left and we could have just kept on drinking without incident. But I was much too heated to allow it to fade away. It didn't take me long to go after him.

The inside of his bungalow was laid out differently from ours. It was clean and had a small foyer with an end table and chair. I remember looking down and seeing a book opened and some magazines on the floor.

"I order you to get the fuck out of my bungalow, asshole," he demanded. "Are you fucking marines stupid? Don't they teach you what orders are out there on the base?"

"Why are *you* such an asshole?" I moved in close. "You have no right coming into our bungalow shouting out orders. We weren't bothering you. In fact, we never bother anybody."

At that point we were so close to each other that I didn't see his hands rise to push me away from him. The instant he made contact with my chest everything went to hell. He might have hit me once but after that he spent most of the time catching blows. I never should have picked up the end table and busted it over his head. It was enough to land him in the hospital for a few days.

I left when he was down. I have no idea how he got to the hospital or who found him. I just went back to my bungalow and kept drinking.

The following Friday night John Kaiser and I were just about to head out to a bar in Waikiki when the Navy Shore Patrol stopped us. They asked us our names and our MOS, our military occupation specialties. That was really all they were looking for. Seconds after we answered they arrested Corporal John Kaiser and me for assault and battery. I don't have a clue why it took them so long to arrest us.

The navy brig sucked. They held us until Monday morning in these 3' by 6' cells with a small toilet and no sink. It was the monotony that drove me crazy. If I could have talked to Kaiser, played cards, or told stories about home it would have been easier. But I never could get used to solitary confinement.

On Monday morning, around six, a Marine Corps officer came to get us. He wasn't pleased. He brought us back to Kona and told us to report to the major and make ourselves more presentable. We looked and smelled pretty bad after a weekend with no shave and no shower. The major told us that the assault and battery charges were court-martial offenses. I was numb when he said that the Marine Corps would provide us both with defense attorneys.

The last thing I'd ever wanted to happen was to be drummed out of the Marine Corps. I just couldn't even consider going back to the old Mullen guys if that happened. If I arrived in Southie with a dishonorable discharge it would be like having a scarlet *D* branded on my back for everybody to see. I just couldn't face it. I woke up every morning thinking about the upcoming trial.

I'd been given a secret clearance when I got stationed in Hawaii. I don't know how or why it happened. Not everybody got it, and it meant absolutely nothing to me at the time. I'd stand at the door and check identification or walk the perimeter every time there was a regimental meeting; I'd hear things I never should have heard until later down the line.

Sometime after our release from the navy brig the meetings became more frequent. I'd pick up information about troops being deployed. I overheard the generals talking directly about Vietnam. It was clear as day; we were going to send more troops overseas.

One day I happened to overhear that a decision had been made to let everybody out of the brig who wasn't a murderer and ship them all overseas — all those who were awaiting a court-martial would be cleared and given a rifle and a ticket to 'Nam. I was thrilled — I no longer had to be concerned that I'd be disgraced by a dishonorable discharge and be ashamed to be back in Southie. But at nineteen years old I had no idea what was about to happen to me.

7. A WAR WE SHOULD HAVE WON

I want to make my views about the war perfectly clear. I went to Vietnam in 1965. The war was just beginning to heat up. I did not experience the Vietnam that my fellow marines encountered from 1967 to 1969. Those marines took most of the heat. I'm no war hero. I may have received medals for being "in country," but so did every other soldier who stepped foot into Vietnam.

The 4th Marine Brigade shipped out of Pearl Harbor and landed at Hue. My brigade landed further north. Our ship headed up the Perfume River, and even though we were in friendly territory, this was a full assault landing; we were locked and loaded, ready to hit the beach. I remember feeling my gut tight with anxiety. The emerald green foliage that shielded the river's banks seemed to ooze tropical sounds. New smells — pungent, powerful aromas — overwhelmed our olfactory senses, heightening the intensity of what was about to happen. Some marines looked like they might be praying. We were just kids, and what we'd seen of what we were about to do came from film of assault landings during World War II.

Finally the command came to hit the beach. But instead of being met by a volley of bullets, as my memory serves me there was a South Vietnamese band playing the Marines Corps hymn by way of welcome. The heat made my helmet feel heavy, and beads of sweat ran down my back. I wasn't quite sure whether the loss of bodily fluid was due to the conditions, the weight of my gear and my flak jacket, or the subconscious knowledge that an army out in that jungle somewhere was going to try to take my life over the next twelve months.

Our brigade mounted up right away and humped to Phu Bai. Our immediate responsibility was to secure the airport and "settle in" without settling in. We had to set up battalion areas for command and operations, but securing the perimeter would be the key to our survival. The darkness in Vietnam was your enemy; it was darkness so deep and black that when you blinked there was no significant color change. It was truly black as night.

We dug a 360-degree defensive perimeter around the airport and erected razor-sharp wire to keep out the Viet Cong. In the event that the VC were crafty enough to cut through the wire our boys had a little welcoming party waiting. First they laid wire connected to trip flares. The instant the flares fired into the air it took away Charlie's protective cover of darkness. Immediately the perimeter would convert from midnight black to an umbrella of daylight. And if the VC got past the flares, there'd be another trip wire several feet inside the perimeter attached to claymore mines laid every fifty yards. Claymores spray 3,200 pieces of razor-sharp U.S steel at 2,800 feet per second. Anything in a 180-degree arc within an area of 50 yards would be reduced to mash. Or at the very least, it wouldn't be walking away.

Some guys referred to the Viet Cong as "Mr. Charles" or "Charlie"; whatever you called them, the little guys with slanty eyes were trying to keep me from returning to Southie.

The weather in Vietnam was another enemy. During the day we'd build little shelters we could call home, protection from the sun and cover from the rain. Monsoon season started in October. It was like being underwater twenty-four hours a day: for six to eight weeks you'd be wet from head to toe. Your boots and socks would rot. I had trouble with the skin on my feet turning wrinkly white and peeling off. The continuous sheets of rain turned the earth into a rancid shit field.

The summer temperatures in Vietnam easily rose to 115 degrees during the day with absolutely no wind. The heat was so thick it would cling to you. And the higher your altitude, the more it felt as though the heat was forcing your lungs closed, cutting off your oxygen supply. But you still had to move if you wanted to stay alive. Charlie never took a day off in Vietnam. He was accustomed to the heat from birth.

After twenty minutes of humping with a rifle, ammunition, a backpack with rations, and several canteens of water, your sweat would dry up and it would feel as though ammonia was trying to burn a path through every pore in your skin. None of us carried the sixty-pound backpacks we'd trained with on Parris Island. We just carried the basics — no more than twenty pounds. We'd eat salt tablets to retain fluid, but really there was nothing to get the human body through these extremes — guys still passed out from exhaustion.

Our first night patrol outside of Phu Bai was filled with nothing short of breathtaking fear. We had no idea what to expect. My fixed position was in a foxhole about forty yards from the woods line. I'd just dug two little holes below the sandbags, placing my hand grenades in one and my illumination grenades in another. Although the air around me was pitch black, I wanted to know exactly where my frags were if things got busy. Out of nowhere I heard the distinct rat-tat-tat of a Russian AK-47 cutting through the night. It must have been a hundred yards from my position. Instantly I heard return fire from our guys. I sat up on the edge of my foxhole watching the tracers run across the black blanket covering the jungle.

Suddenly Corporal Tiser from New Orleans realized that the incoming rifle fire was being directed over our heads, and we immediately rolled back into our foxholes. We'd never been shot at before. But it's funny — the first time it happened all the anxiety and pent-up fear rushed out of me. I reacted. You just react. Everything I was taught at Parris Island kicked in, just like it's supposed to.

Before the sun went down the next day I'd finished writing to my mother and father. In 1965 people at home weren't yet saturated by coverage of the effort in Vietnam. Kids were leaving in body bags, but not to such an extent that the media focused their attention on it the way they would two and three years later. I wrote my mother that I was on an extended vacation in an exotic land, in a nice country with nice people. I didn't want her to worry about me.

Although I spent nine months in Vietnam, much of what I experienced there has been erased by time and by memories of the war I tried to help win in Northern Ireland. But there are a few specific episodes from my stay that shaped my character as a soldier and strengthened my belief in destiny.

Let me tell you those stories that have followed me through all these years.

The terrain in South Vietnam made it difficult for us to find the VC. Where I was, up north, the hills were broken up by flat, sandy, unused fields. From any given position we were either encompassed by a valley or surrounded by hills. We had no choice but to climb, descend, and hump. And Charlie could be anywhere.

One afternoon in the heat of July we ran out of water while our company was out on patrol. I'm not sure exactly how long we'd been out or what our particular mission was that day, other than the obvious — hunting the Viet Cong. For some reason we weren't able to get a helicopter to resupply our water.

Suddenly a helicopter landed on a hill only a few kilometers away to take a wounded marine back for medical care. I can still see the first lieutenant calling up on the radio and asking for help.

"Nee, grab three men and get on that chopper," he barked.

I'm not sure why he picked me, but we humped it to that chopper, hopped on, and headed back to Phu Bai. There they had a six-by truck gassed up with a driver, and a marine riding shotgun inside the front cab. We headed right over to the water buffalo —

big water tanks — and filled up as many five-gallon canisters as we could fit inside the truck. I knew the way out, so I sat behind the driver while the three marines I'd come with each took a corner position in the back of the truck.

Right outside Phu Bai, just beyond a dirt road with sand enbankments, was Hill 180, where a platoon of marines had dug in. As we passed Hill 180 our six-by entered an open road. The view was picturesque — dark green rolling hills to our right and a wide-open plain of rice paddies in front of us. It's amazing how such a beautiful place can swallow your attention. The last thing on any of our minds at that moment was dying.

Bam!

My memory has it happening in slow motion, but I'm sure you don't float through the air when you hit a land mine. We were actually inside the explosion. I remember being thrown up in the air and feeling my helmet stripped off my head by the blast. Everything went silent when I landed back inside the six-by.

"Hold your positions! Hold your positions," I managed, not knowing who was alive or dead.

The water cans were scattered all over the road and the truck was now at a right angle. I leaned to look inside the cab of the truck. Both men were pretty messed up. The driver was hunched over the steering wheel and moaning. I saw blood on the Marine riding shotgun. He was unconscious, but there wasn't enough blood for me to think he was dead. I knew enough about the effects of being inside a blast: it saves you from the tiny razor-sharp steel of the land mine but the concussion itself can kill.

I immediately saw that my three guys were alive and not in trouble. I wasn't too keen on getting down on the road in case there were more mines there. I saw the marines on the hill to our right were making their way to assist us. They stopped on the edge of the road and called for a medevac helicopter to transport the guys inside the cab.

I decided to take one of the marines and get down on the road. We crawled about 70 or 80 yards on our bellies, probing the road with our bayonets while our comrades transported the wounded. I think the first lieutenant from the group of the marines road-side called us back to help us push the disabled truck off the road. Another six-by had already been sent from Phu Bai. We grabbed the five-gallon water canisters that hadn't been damaged, loaded them on the truck, and headed back to our company.

When I think back on it, it's amazing we all weren't killed that day. I lost my hearing for a few days and another marine had a surface cut on his leg. It must have been my mother's prayers that got me through.

Whenever I think about casualties I recall two images that are seared into my consciousness. The first casualty occurred during an operation to burn out some caves on the side of a hill just north of Phu Bai. I'm not sure whether anybody was inside the caves, but reports had come in suggesting that Charlie was using the caves to plan attacks. The helicopter pilots were remarkable — they'd get us to within four or five feet of a drop zone and then we'd jump out and head for cover.

The choppers we used back then were small; you could only comfortably fit three or four men inside. Some marines had already landed and taken their positions around the caves. I could see them waiting as our chopper approached our drop zone. Corporal Blaylock had the flamethrower attached to his back and Eddie Diamond was carrying the M60 machine gun that would be used for cover.

It could have been the fault of aerodynamics, or maybe the pilot just snuck too close to the hill and was adjusting his altitude. But on this particular day the chopper veered sharply left at the same instant that Blaylock, Eddie, and I jumped. We missed the crest of the hill and jumped into the slope. I was lucky: the ground I hit was loose. I just started to slide down the side of the hill. But Corporal Blaylock didn't have fortune on his side that day; he landed on a *punji* stick — a bamboo pole sharpened to a point — that pierced right through the center of his spine. Charlie used punji sticks as booby traps in all types of terrain. Sometimes they'd put poison on the end to inflict more damage.

Blaylock didn't scream; I think he was in deep shock. I'll never forget the emptiness of his stare as we pulled him off the stick. I was young and didn't think much about it back then. My job was to get the flamethrower off his back and complete our mission. I could see two cave openings to my right; Eddie laid down suppression fire into the mouths of the caves while I came around to the right and emptied fire straight on. Everything inside had to burn.

We took no fire during the mission, so the caves may have been empty. Blaylock was going home, paralyzed for life.

Another memory is that of a young marine with black hair and olive skin who was no older than twenty. I happened to be back at base and heading to see one of my wounded friends inside the medical tents. Some choppers had just flown in casualties from a firefight. As I entered the front of the tent one of the corpsmen asked for a hand. The kid on his stretcher had a gaping, sucking chest wound shaped like an S. He saw me looking at his wound. I couldn't help it. The noise haunts me sometimes — it was a hiss like a child sipping the last of his soda through a straw. The blood bubbled in small round circles that broke apart as they hit the air. For an instant we could read each other's thoughts. He knew that I knew he was dying.

The most absurd thing that ever happened to me in Vietnam could easily have sent me home in a body bag. One night I went out with a group to ambush Charlie. The lieutenant showed me a map where the ARVN — the Army of the Republic of Vietnam — reported nighttime enemy activity. I grabbed L.A. Ducks, a hilarious black kid from Watts; Corporal Korpshiski from Chicago (we called him Ski); Big Willy Walker, a black marine from Chicago; and a new boot who'd just arrived. We took him along to get a taste of action.

The activity was between Hill 180 and Hill 220. We left at dusk. You always moved just before the sky went black; the hills forever cast shadows and it took a while for your eyes to adjust to the sheer darkness of the Vietnam countryside. We left camp surreptitiously, marching quietly past an ARVN base off to our left. Our position was just over a wooden footbridge that crossed a large swampy area. On the other side of the bridge was a trail where the activity had been spotted. We set up an ambush just below a slight rise in the trail.

I stationed the new guy on our side of the bridge, far back from the crest of the trail. Willy Walker and L.A. Ducks went to the left while Ski and I positioned ourselves on the right. It was a perfect ambush; nothing could survive inside our coverage area. We settled in for the evening in positions that covered everything going or coming over the bridge in a 45-degree field of fire.

At 4 A.M. the stillness of the night was shattered by the chilling ring of a cheap alarm clock. I usually checked my men before heading out, but who would have figured some soldier would bring an alarm clock on an ambush? I couldn't see the reaction on anybody else's face, but I know mine was a cross between abject fear and complete surprise. The blanket of darkness was so thick you couldn't see your pecker when you pissed. Now a goddamn alarm clock was broadcasting our position to the Viet Cong! I heard L.A. Ducks cursing to himself as the crunching sound of the butt of his rifle smashed against the ringing bell.

"Just turn it off," I whispered.

All of us were totally exposed and had to scramble back over the bridge. We leapfrogged back one at time, picked up the new guy, and headed into the brush. We set up a defensive semicircle facing the positions we had just retreated from. We were just as concerned about the ARVN behind us, because they spooked easily and would shoot at anything after dark. I think we sat there until the light of day came on hard.

I'll never forget telling the first lieutenant the story. "What went off?" he laughed. The thought of L.A. Ducks bringing a wake-up call to an ambush was funny after we were all safe and sound.

I've always been amazed at how many potentially deadly situations in my life have turned out in my favor; a young Marine could go out at night to take a piss and only pieces of him would be sent back to his family.

My return from Vietnam was anticlimactic. I didn't get any "baby killer" accusations lobbed at me. I returned to Southie, a place that has always welcomed marines with open arms. I've heard that Southie lost seven times the national average, per capita, for men killed in combat in all the wars Americans have fought.

The way we exited Vietnam was shameful. I was sick to my stomach the day I watched Saigon fall on television. I was ashamed to be part of it all. I blame politicians and the media for what happened to us in Vietnam. There is no doubt in my mind — Vietnam was a war we could have won.

8. CRIME PAYS

I came back home from Vietnam at the end of January, 1966. After thirty days' leave I had to fulfill my obligation to the Marine Corps by serving a little over seven months at Camp Elmore in Norfolk, Virginia. I was released from the Marines with an honorable discharge in October 1966.

Southie hadn't changed much since my departure. The Mullens were still stealing, tailgating all the truck stops in the warehouse areas of Southie, A Street, B Street, and C Street. The waterfront still provided the Mullens plenty of tuna, crabmeat, and whatever was coming in from Europe: electronic equipment, radios, televisions, stereos.

I moved in with my parents when I returned from active duty. They were now living at the corner of O and Third Streets. There were a lot of possibilities suddenly available to me; I remember feeling a little disoriented making my way back into "normal" life. It felt as though time was passing in a different way. For one thing I wasn't in the Marine Corps anymore, and that took a bit of adjusting to. With all of the restrictions to your personal freedom that it entailed, life as a marine in Vietnam was so different from that of a civilian, and the transition was jarring. That's the only way I can describe it.

I had no idea how I was going to make a living. The *Boston Globe* was in Dorchester, only minutes from my house. My family knew several of the men who worked on their printing presses, all of them from Ireland, and one of those men vouched for me. That wasn't too much of a stretch for him; after all, I was an honorably discharged marine returning from combat in Vietnam. The game plan was to first get me employed as a custodian; the Irish guys told me I'd get into the printer's union within six months.

Being a custodian wasn't something I liked. I'm not putting the job down; I just didn't particularly enjoy mopping and sweeping. But I stuck with it because a printer's pay was very good for somebody who hadn't finished high school, the benefits were excellent, and it was a legitimate future. I had to start somewhere.

As fate would have it, however, the head of maintenance was a pure asshole. He was maybe fifty years old, a small man with shifty brown eyes who seemed to always watch you, just waiting to catch you screwing up so he could bark out instructions on "procedure." He was the type of guy who always told you how you could have done things better after you'd finished the job — if he'd told you how to do it right before you started, he couldn't yell at you later. A lot of the custodians at the *Globe* were older Irish guys who had had to leave Ireland out of financial desperation and were willing to take any job in order to make ends meet. Lobel, the head maintenance guy, knew this and was particularly hard on the Irish guys. He forced them to work longer hours than was required. He was always threatening to replace some worker or another with somebody who'd do a better job. Because there was no real union he was able to get away with keeping them on edge, keeping them anxious about losing their jobs.

For nearly six months I watched him disrespect my people. Then one day I got tired of watching how he treated the Irish. I was mopping a corridor near Lobel's office. I was in a bad mood and just happened to catch the tail end of one of his threats as he walked past me. I kept my head down but followed him to his office, mop in hand. He sat down at his desk and never saw it coming. I whacked him right across the face with the wet mop. In fact, I was surprised how the impact knocked him off his chair. I immediately sat on him and the fear in his eyes told me I owned him.

"I know I'm gonna lose my job over this, but if you don't

change your attitude toward the old Irish guys and start treating them as human beings, I'll come back and hit you with a baseball bat in the parking lot. And like that mop, you'll never see it coming, you prick."

He got the point, and I was asked to resign. It didn't really matter to me. I was young; I had no kids and no real responsibilities. I felt I'd done the right thing: Lobel had no right bullying those working men like that. It wasn't as though they could file a grievance — they had no union. The way I saw it, given Lobel's entrenched, cruel attitude, I couldn't send him a Hallmark card. I had to get his attention.

But it didn't end there. I knew I had to follow up, to reinforce the lesson and make sure Lobel knew my word was good. The *Globe* had an open cafeteria and I knew exactly when the Irish guys and Lobel would be eating. I made it a point to make an appearance at least once a month. The first thing I'd do was pull up a chair to Lobel's table and ask him how he was doing. "Fine," he'd always respond. Then I'd push my chair in and go eat lunch with the Irish guys. "He's been very good to us lately, Pat," they'd say. Not one of them ever told me another story about old Lobel bullying someone. That made my time at the *Globe* worth every minute. Maybe Lobel eventually saw the error of his ways. These were good men, good workers who deserved a break.

My next job was with the Laborers. I never worked with my father, but I was on the job with some of his friends. Laboring was hard work, but it was regular hours and decent pay. Then on the weekends I'd be out with the usual crowd. And it didn't take me long to notice that most of my Mullen gang cronies slept in on weekday mornings, while I was up at 6 A.M. And they always had more money in their pockets than I did. I didn't have any college education, but I certainly wasn't stupid. Something didn't jive. I busted my hump all week, and on the weekends these guys would have five or six times more money in their pocket. Don't get me wrong — the Mullens always spread their money around — but I felt awkward always spending all my money before Friday night was over.

One morning I woke up tired and sore. "The hell with this," I thought. I could make a choice. I had other options. Such as stealing.

My progression into crime was as natural as a baby's transition from crawling to walking. I didn't have an epiphany; I never sat down and had a soul-searching experience in which I decided that being a criminal was my goal in life. It just seemed natural — there was a lot of money to be had if you spent the time planning jobs right. The more I hung with the Mullens, the easier it was to go out on jobs. I'd simply ask if they needed another guy.

The Hotel Essex was the score that taught me that crime pays very well. It was a modest businessmen's hotel, nothing fancy, but it was pretty busy because South Station was directly across the street. Trains came every hour with businessmen from all over the country. Most would only stay a day or two and move on. Back then we lived in a cash economy; some people used credit cards for some transactions, but nothing like the extent to which credit cards are used today. The Essex had a restaurant and lounge that was always packed with a mix of businessmen and locals. Most of my Mullen gang buddies were of legal drinking age by this point. I liked the hotel's location; it was on the outskirts of Southie but close enough that I could get back home quickly if I had to. Several of us hung out at the Essex lounge on Friday nights. But we never imagined the Hotel Essex would become a target.

It happened by accident. Jerry Roake, Jimmy Mantville, and I were eating breakfast in the restaurant one morning and the idea just jumped out at us. It was Monday, the day the armored truck showed up to transport the weekend receipts. Two armed guards met the manager in the lobby and — we later learned — were escorted to a fourth-floor office. In five minutes the guards would walk off the elevators and into the lobby carrying bags of money that seemed to float by us in tantalizingly slow motion. On the day we conjured the idea, nobody had to say anything: we looked at each other, all bright eyes and sinister smiles. The second the bags of money left our view and the guards exited the front lobby we turned to each other, chuckling with anticipation at our latest job and the money we'd make off it. The bulge in those bags had turned the Hotel Essex into the Mullens' next target.

We watched the hotel every Monday for two months, both from inside the resturant and from a building across the street. The pattern of the pickup was identical each time, like clockwork. As a thief you love that trait in people because you know they're dependable: they're always in the same place at the same time. Our job in those two months was to time our activities around theirs. Our surveillance told us that the hotel bookkeeper would arrive at 8:55 A.M. She'd get a coffee and go straight to her fourth-floor office. She'd disable the alarms, open the door, step inside, and reactivate the alarms. At 9:30 A.M. the armored car would pull close to the front door, and just as on the first day we'd seen them, the guards would be met and escorted by the manager to the fourth floor. Sometime between 9:33 and 9:35 the two guards would enter the office and pick up the receipts.

At first we thought about breaking into the office late on a Sunday night, before the guards arrived for the pickup. But the place was bugged. Each pane of glass in the windows held a small detection device wired to the windowsill. Every door was wired as well. And if that wired connection was broken at any point, an alarm would alert hotel management and possibly an alarm company or the Boston police. We didn't have the technical knowledge at that time to shut down the alarm system, so we had to come up with another plan.

We started watching the guards to see if there was any area within their hotel route where they might be vulnerable to a quick hit. But nothing came of it; we'd never have enough time to disarm them, subdue them, and secure the money.

Weeks and weeks marched by with no real plan emerging, but I didn't want to give up.

The break came one Friday evening when I was across from the Hotel Essex in a building next to South Station that had been partially closed off due to construction. Day or night I could enter the building from the rear and climb to the top floor. The offices weren't locked. I had binoculars, and I could actually see the money being counted in the fourth-floor office in the hotel. Sometimes I'd sit alone just thinking, timing the guards, and plotting how to make that money ours. On this particular evening I noticed that a window in the fourth-floor office was ajar. It couldn't have been bugged. Either somebody had messed up or it had been deliberately left open for ventilation.

Being the weekend, we had a few days to act. That Sunday evening, using an alias, Gerry rented a room for the night on the fourth floor of the hotel. We got lucky: the room happened to be close to the office we'd been casing. Gerry had the keys to the hotel room, and our job was to float in whenever things felt right. It was normal to see Jimmy and me traipsing through the lobby, but Gerry liked to stay in Southie and, as a consequence, nobody knew him. He brought a suitcase with guns, gloves, masks, and duct tape.

Inside the hotel room Gerry and Jimmy turned on the television while I napped. After the bars closed, around 2 A.M., I opened the window in our hotel room and climbed out on the ledge. It had to be at least fifty feet down to the pavement. Thank God the ledge was a healthy twelve to eighteen inches across. Gerry and Jimmy followed, and we inched our way slowly toward the office. We were all dressed in black, including the gloves on our hands, and I carried a small gym bag with tape and three guns.

This is what noncriminals can't fathom. "Why the hell would you risk arrest, or worse, falling to your death, just for money? Just get a job!" they think. But that's what separates us from you. We love risk — it's that simple. We live for it. Risk makes us feel alive. As I stood on that ledge that night gulping in deep breaths of air, I could feel the hairs on my head standing up. The warm air swirled around my face as I suppressed the panic in my brain. The fear of falling was trumped by the thrill of tiptoeing on a ledge fifty feet above ground, inside the Boston skyline. Flirting with death to score some cash: this was what I lived for.

I squatted carefully, my back to the window, until I had the bottom of the wooden window snug in the palms of my hands. Slowly I rose, listening for any noise that would signal a break in the window's sensor wires. The window was safe. I climbed in quickly and Gerry and Jimmy followed me. I closed the window all the way. This is something we had discussed in the planning stage: should we leave the window slightly ajar, as it was, or should we close it, as it should have been? I figured that the open window had to have been a mistake, because on every other surveillance it had been closed. The assumption we made was that it was an oversight on an employee's part, and that if we returned the window to that open position and it was seen, we'd risk unwanted attention, because it should have been closed in the first place.

Once inside we scouted the room, found the safe, and planned our morning strategy. There were two doors and two sets of alarms; the bookkeeper opened both doors and disarmed both alarms before going to work. It was going to be easy. We'd taken notes on the bookkeeper: she was fifty-five, pear shaped. She looked kindly. She'd cooperate.

We waited in that room for seven hours. Nobody spoke. Nobody yawned. Nobody slept. Gerry and Jimmy sat on the floor with their guns resting in their laps; they'd pulled their masks up on top of their heads because they were itchy. They didn't take them off because they wanted to pull the masks down quickly when the time came. The only thing that disrupted the silence in the room was the ticking clock on the wall. Every once in a while we'd hear somebody moving around out in the hallway, people entering a room nearby, and my heart would pick up a few beats. But for the most part all I could see were the white circles of Gerry and Jimmy's faces.

At 8:57 A.M. we heard keys jingling and the alarm buttons being pushed. It was time. Quietly we stood and pulled our masks down. As soon as the bookkeeper closed the second door and entered the office, I stuck my gun in her face.

She turned ghost-white, dropped her coffee, and clutched her heart. All I could think was, "Shit, this lady is gonna have a heart attack." She was hyperventilating and her lips turned purple. She started to buckle and I put my arm around her waist to keep her upright.

"Shit," Gerry whispered. "No bookkeeper, no safe!"

I couldn't let the poor lady die of a heart attack — so I put my .38 on the desk and let her lean on me. I gently put her in the nearest seat.

"You'll be alright," I said. "Don't worry. Nothing is going to happen to you."

Her color wasn't returning and her breathing was still shallow. "Fuck!" I screamed in my mind. "This can't be fucking happening!" I was there to steal, not put an old lady in an early grave. I straightened her up in the chair. "Sit still; I'll get you some water," I told her. I quickly grabbed a cup from the shelf nearby and filled it at the water cooler. Jimmy stood by the safe, eyes darting around the office. She took a drink and Gerry came over, as concerned as I was. He'd wet some paper towels and draped them over her wrists.

"I'm scared. I'm scared," she said.

"Don't worry. It's going to be okay. Just relax," I urged. "We're just here for the safe, the money. That's all. We won't hurt you, miss." I was so concerned about her surviving the robbery I was being too nice. And it was about to bite me in the ass.

"The guns frighten me. Please put away those guns." In any other robbery this request would have been absurd, but I was afraid for her life.

"Okay," I said, "we'll put away the guns."

Gerry spun toward us, his eyes expressing a combination of anger and disbelief. "What the fuck are you doing?" Gerry hissed. "This is a fuckin' robbery! Remember!"

Jimmy never budged or said anything. He just kept watching for anyone else approaching. Later on I would congratulate him on his discipline.

"Okay, I'll put the gun away, but if I do that you have to do me a favor," I said.

"What favor, honey?" she asked. I wasn't aware of it in the heat of the moment, but this old lady was pretty crafty.

"You gotta open the safe," I came right back.

"No," she said, and she said it firmly. I couldn't believe what I was hearing! Here she was, on the verge of a heart attack, and she was being defiant! Oh, but she wasn't done: "I'm not going to do that." And she said that with even more conviction!

"Why? You gotta open the safe," I said, still being nice. Incredulous, but still nice.

"No, I don't have to," she said.

I guess my body language was asking "why" because this is how she answered: "Because you're a nice boy and I know you won't shoot me." She wasn't being arrogant or cocky. She just seemed to believe in the importance of her job — keeping the money safe — and she believed that because I was so well mannered we'd just forget about our plan. She had me figured right, but not Gerry. He stomped over and immediately pushed the gun barrel into the side of her temple. He hissed softly, "Oh, he's nice, but I'll blow your fucking brains out." Of course Gerry was bluffing, but he was giving a performance worthy of *Reservoir Dogs*. She turned and looked at me.

I nodded. And my nod said: "He ain't nice, miss. He'll shoot you." She bought it. Hell, I bought it! Gerry was fucking spooky.

She gulped and started to rise from her seat. I helped her. Funny, she seems fine now, I thought. I was so relieved. She opened the safe. I then guided her back to a chair, even though she didn't need the help. I smiled as Jimmy and Gerry loaded stacks of cash into the gym bag. I felt wonderful. Even though it was never our intention to hurt anybody and the old bookkeeper had put that to the test, we came out of it. Gerry's performance was what did it.

We had less than twenty minutes to get out before the guards came. But the bookkeeper was calm and the bag was being filled. So no panic; there was time. The whole room was full of a wild energy.

The bags filled, we got ready to get the hell out of Dodge. The only thing we needed to do was to tie up the bookkeeper. I figured after the scare Gerry had put into her she'd go along easy. And given that, I probably should have let Gerry secure her.

"Okay miss, I have to tape your arms to the chair and put one little piece over your mouth," I said.

She grabbed her heart again. I groaned immediately, "Here we go again."

"Please, I'll die. Don't tape my mouth."

"If I don't, you've got to promise not to peek," I told her.

Gerry had enough. "Peek! Promise you won't peek!" Gerry had raised his voice a bit. "What, are you outta your fuckin' mind?! Give me the tape."

"I promise I won't peek," she jumped in. "I will not turn around even for a second. I promise!"

"Lower your fucking voice, lady. 'Promise?' Shit. This is a fuckin' robbery," Gerry growled at her. "How's this? I promise I won't shoot you in the head if you shut the fuck up." Gerry turned to me. "Put the tape on her."

I couldn't help but admire her. She wasn't stupid or dense; I could tell she believed in doing her job. She had guts. She probably had a big family at home, maybe even some grandchildren. Gerry moved toward the door — we had planned to walk out of the hotel with those bags of money, not climb back out onto the ledge — so once Gerry had turned away I didn't seal her mouth fully, and I taped her wrists to the chair so loosely she could raise and lower her arms a good twelve inches. I put her in the corner, face to the wall, and we tucked our guns into the gym bags.

"Okay, we're taking our masks off now. Remember you promised not to peek, miss. Do not turn around."

"I won't peek. I promised," she responded sincerely.

"This is fuckin' crazy! Playing peek-a-fucking-boo with this old broad!" Jimmy finally whispered.

"I trust her. She won't peek," I said. And she didn't.

We opened the door and stepped out with confidence. I believe I was the last guy inside so I left one glove on to close the door behind me. Fingerprints, you know. Halfway down the corridor I slipped the glove into my pocket. We took the stairway exit — less chance of running into anybody who might be able to identify us later. We didn't run, move fast, or look anxious. All of us wore regular clothes so we moved naturally, chatting, as if we belonged there. At the bottom of the stairs we exited the side door, got into Buddy's car, and drove away.

"How did it go?" Buddy asked.

"Fucking great. I thought Pat was gonna cut the lady in. Make her a full partner," Jimmy said.

"I promise I won't peek," Gerry jumped in, trying to imitate the lady's voice.

Everybody laughed as we headed back toward Southie. But I believed her when she said she wouldn't turn around. It was my intuition and I was proved right. The bookkeeper was interviewed the next day in the *Boston Herald*. She said (of course, I'm paraphrasing), "Two of them were thugs, but one of them was such a nice young man." I laughed when I read it to Gerry and Jimmy. "Well if we get caught," I said, "you guys are going to jail for a long time. You're thugs! Mean, nasty, no-mannered thugs!" I was howling.

There was more than thirty thousand dollars in the safe. The following Friday we were all back at the Hotel Essex bar, just like a normal Friday night. But now we were planning our next heist — oh, and celebrating the past week's haul! Nobody suspected us. It was so well done, so well executed. I was proud that we hadn't hurt that slippery old lady, that we had gotten our money and gotten away.

I couldn't wait to do it again.

9. PETER NEE

In 1969 my brother Peter — a sweet, tough, smart kid and a better son to his parents than I ever was — was murdered, shot twice in the face. Just twenty-two, he'd survived two tours in Vietnam only to be killed in his hometown. Imagine being in 'Nam; surviving a vicious, determined enemy; looking forward to coming home, and then being killed two months after your return.

Peter's death changed everything for me. I've never been the same since the night I saw him on that slab in the morgue. I know firsthand how the death of a sibling changes the lives of the rest of the family. It's not just pain and grief; positive changes can also come in death's wake. You all appreciate life more. When you lose someone you love you realize life's capricious nature.

But there was a distinct element in Peter's death: Peter didn't just die. He was murdered. And that changed me from a marine veteran who killed the enemy and a Mullen who stole for the money and the thrill to something else. In the shadow of Peter's death I became more intense, more serious. The resolve I felt when I shot Grumpy Grondin with that arrow, the resolve I showed in Marine Corps boot camp and then in combat in Vietnam, it was that resolve that hardened in me as I wept. I heard my heart speak the words: "Peter, I will avenge you!"

I cried over Peter like I had never cried before. I had never called Peter my "little" brother — until he died, that is. He was bigger, tougher, more barrel-chested, and better looking than me. And to add the ultimate Southie insult, he could kick my ass. Not in grammar school, of course, but by middle school and high school, when he had put some height and weight on, he could kick my ass. With Peter having the same mindset as me, I was screwed. At one point I remember thinking (but never told him) "Man, I'm lucky you're my brother!"

Still, there were ways in which Peter and I were quite different. He had a mild temperament; he never started any problems. I found problems, and even if I didn't start them, they found me. Peter was blessed with a personality that didn't invite hostility. But if you crossed the line with him you found out quickly that his resolve matched his size. Nobody ever doubted his courage.

Peter and I were close. I was the older brother by a year. In fact, Peter and I teamed up for a lot of fights when we first arrived in Southie. Our other brothers, Michael and Sean, were young and never had to do any of that type of stuff to gain acceptance. Peter made my mother and father proud. He was just a good-hearted kid, a great son. After he was killed, when no one was around to see me, I cried for him because he was no longer with us. But I also cried for myself and my loss; I cried so much and so hard I didn't think I'd ever stop crying.

Peter had served with the Air Force Strategic Air Command throughout Vietnam. When he came home he got a fantastic job at the Boston Liquor Distributors and was just beginning the next phase of his life. We all lived at home back then and I remember Peter sharing every paycheck with my parents. And I'll never forget how much he loved to party!

One night Peter was at the Coachman Bar at I and Broadway in Southie drinking beers with a few close friends. Like Peter, some of them had served in Vietnam and had been back in Southie for only a few months. There was a heated argument between another bar patron and Peter's friends. From what I was told Peter wasn't involved in the argument, but his friends were — which, for a Southie guy, meant that he was nevertheless in the fray.

For the uninitiated, let me explain: A man backs up a friend when the friend is in the right. That's easy to understand. But a friend also backs up a friend even when the friend is in the wrong. After all, he's a friend, and you're not a referee. He could be dead wrong, but you still have to back him. Drunk, wrong, or both, friends back up friends. And that's what Peter did.

I have no clue as to how everything really played out. All I know is who killed my little brother.

Apparently the argument was about nothing except personalities and too many beers. This was not unusual in Southie, and in Southie everybody takes sides. And taking sides exacts a price. My brother was loyal and stood up for a Mullen. The fight, involving maybe a dozen guys, spilled out into the street. Two of them, Tommy Murphy and Kevin Daley, left all pissed off. Tommy went up the street, brought a gun down from his house, and handed it to Kevin. The fight came to a head on the corner of I and Fourth. Kevin shot the small .22 caliber randomly and continuously. Peter got hit twice in the face, and our friend Bobby took a bullet in the back while he was running away.

I'll never forget the ring of that one phone call. It was two or three o'clock in the morning; we lived in a small apartment, so the phone woke everybody up. Michael was in Vietnam and Sean was home on leave. My mother took the call. My sister Barbara was twelve. "Pat, wake up," Sean sobbed as he stepped into my room. I was sitting up already. I looked at him: he was crying, in near shock. "Peter's been shot," he blurted. A chill ran through me. I was stunned. Peter was a pure citizen, a working guy. Who would shoot him? And why? He was so well liked. I took the deepest breath I've ever taken in my life. Because I knew, as the oldest, that I'd have to take charge of the situation. I'd have to be strong for mom, dad, and my brothers and sister. Tears began to well, but I forced them back. I had to suppress my emotions — for now anyway. I'd have time to cry, plenty of time. But now I had to support my family.

Dad, Sean, and I headed to the morgue to identify Peter's body. We had left my distraught mother at the house. She was not ready to see her boy dead on a slab. We left her keening by the kitchen table, wailing in lamentation for her son. Keening keeps the banshee away from one's soul. In Ireland it's believed that the banshee stands on the doorstep between life and death; if you hear the banshee's wail, she's here to take your soul. Of course, I knew Peter was gone; his soul had already been taken. But my mother's cries that night penetrated my being like nothing I've ever heard before or since.

I made Dad and Sean wait upstairs. BoBo Conolly, a Boston police officer from Southie, led me down the stairs to the morgue. I couldn't help but think of me and Peter playing stickball in the old schoolyard when we were little kids, or the times we fought as brothers over stupid stuff that didn't amount to anything. I worried about my dad, and I knew my mom would never be the same again.

"Pat, it's Peter," BoBo said. "They got him on the corner of I and Fourth."

He opened the sliding table and a rush of dark cold hit my face. I was numb. I had been hoping it was all a big mistake or a bad dream. I was hoping that BoBo, despite the fact that he knew Peter very well, was wrong.

BoBo peeled back the sheets and there was Peter. The prick had shot him right in the head, one shot right over his left eye and one shot below the eye. I'd seen people dead in Vietnam, but this was my kid brother. Both of the tiny, star-shaped bullet holes were almost closed. I wiped the blood away from his face with my hand. I saw him there lying dead, but his face moved through my memory as crystal-clear snapshots of all the good times we'd had in Southie. I loved this kid. And right then and there I made a promise on his blood. I wanted revenge. I wanted to kill the motherfucker who took my brother and broke my family's heart.

"I'll make this right, Peter," I told him.

I laid the sheet back over him and headed past BoBo. Dad was upstairs. I knew Mike and Sean would take it tough, but they were young and would recover. I was concerned about my dad's reaction. He was such a great father. He'd worked hard all his life, brought his family from poverty in Ireland to the land of opportunity. And now one of his own had two holes in his head. Why Peter? He'd never hurt anyone! It just wasn't fair.

I didn't have to say a word. Dad knew. Sean steadied him under each arm. I cried. We all cried for what Peter would never become. His life had ended needlessly at twenty-two. Dad's body shook as I held him close in my arms. The pain in my chest exploded and my heart split wide open.

I'd seen many things in my life by then, but those small holes in Peter's head did something terrible to my psyche. It was almost as though I floated away from my previous life in that instant and entered a new and darker life. I felt cold inside. When a loved one dies it's devastating — the grief seems endless. But when a loved one is killed you not only have the same crippling grief but you also have a gnawing, relentless drive for revenge, for justice. In time the grief gives way; you reconcile your loss within the confines of the rest of your life. But for me, nothing mattered but revenge. I'll never forget how hard hate came to me that night. I felt like I was drowning in a river and it just felt right to let myself go. Give in to the hate, the drive to kill and make things right. I got sucked under. I had not one moment of doubt that I'd kill whoever had done this to my brother and my family.

"Take Dad home," I told Sean, "I'll be there later."

"Wait for us," Sean said. "We're coming with you."

I paused. Sean was crippled with pain and wanted vengeance. But Dad couldn't afford to lose another son.

"You guys are out. You're too young, Sean, and Dad and Ma need you. I'll handle it from here."

When I eventually got home, most of the Mullens were waiting for me outside. They told me Kevin had killed Peter, and they wanted to go get him immediately. My brain flooded with a silent rage that I couldn't express. I saw Kevin's face in my mind. I saw Peter on the table. The memory of the bullet holes, those star-shaped holes, the blood — it all kept me horribly focused.

"Pat, they're waiting for your word," said Paulie McGonagle, probably the toughest Mullen. A few years older, he was something of a mentor to me. "What do you want to do?" he said.

"No witnesses. We don't help the police," I said. "We'll hold court on the street." Translation: I didn't want the friends who were with Peter to identify Kevin as Peter's killer. I didn't want him arrested — I wanted to kill him. The sad irony was that Kevin was one of us, a true Southie guy and a decorated Vietnam Marine. I'd liked him before this — he was a straight guy. It was Tommy Murphy who was the cause of the whole tragedy — he was a real scumbag, a lowlife drug dealer. But Peter was dead, and I was going to avenge him.

Not surprisingly, Ma was a wreck for several days. The funeral was horrible, but it made my whole family stronger. I held in my grief, and that was hard. How many people know what it's like to need to cry, to express the deepest sorrow, but you have to push it back, keep up a strong front for your family. That's what I did, but it came at great cost. I just felt that if Ma saw me break down it would simply crush her. I felt, right or wrong, that I had to be the rock everyone could come to and rely on. The house was filled with family and friends and somehow that held us all together. At twelve, Barbara didn't quite understand everything; she'd worshipped Peter. Dad just sat alone, very quiet.

One night a few weeks later my father woke me and sat on the edge of my bed. The lines on his face seemed deeper because of the inescapable pain and grief. I knew my Dad, and I knew only one thing could bring him to a better place. Revenge.

"What are you gonna do?" he asked.

I sat up quickly, respectfully. I cleared my throat, rubbed my eyes, took a breath. "I'm gonna hunt him down and kill him."

I'll never forget the pride I saw in my father's eyes in that moment. He didn't smile. He didn't flinch. Right then and there our eyes held one another's soul. I was his oldest son, his right hand. It was as though our love for Peter had joined. I wanted to hold him and tell him everything would be alright. But I knew it would never be okay again.

10. HUNTING

I saw nothing wrong in seeking to avenge my brother's murder. To me the only right thing to do was to kill Kevin. Leave it to the cops? To the law? Forget that. My brother's life was a precious and beautiful thing to my family. Locking Kevin up or putting him to death wasn't going to satisfy my family or me. I had no concern that I was going to become a killer. No, I was an avenger.

It was Peter's murder that turned some of the Mullens from thieves into hunters. I knew and appreciated the fact that certain of the Mullens weren't up to killing. Those guys saw stealing from trains, warehouses, and businesses as perfectly harmless. Stealing was an impersonal act for them, and that was as far as they were willing to go. I never held it against them — they just weren't built for it. And rather than fake it, they were honest: "Pat, we love you, but we're just not up for that kind of thing. Please let us know . . ." I'd stop them; I understood. I shook their hands. They'd always finish up with: "If there's anything else we can do, just ask." And that was heartwarming. I give those guys a lot of credit; they knew their limitations and they were straightforward about it. They didn't try to pretend. And in the situation I was in, I had no patience for phonies who would waste my time. But the rest of the gang was willing to follow me further — enough Mullens stepped up for me to get what I wanted. They were tough, reliable men, men I could count on.

The first thing I'd learned in the Marine Corps was to identify the threat and its capabilities. Well, that was easy; Kevin wasn't in the Killeens or any other organized gang. He was on his own with a loose band of friends.

The second thing to do is formulate a plan of action. I had to kill

Kevin where I wouldn't be seen, or at the very least, where I couldn't be recognized.

Third, I needed to begin a reconnaissance of Kevin's schedule, activities, and habits, and to find the places he frequented. For weeks a full team watched every step Kevin took in Southie. We watched him for more than six months. Each morning I'd sit at the breakfast table and my mother would hover as she watched me write facts about Kevin's locations and movement into a notebook. And then she'd stop moving. I felt her presence, her pure demand for vengeance. "Well . . . are you gonna get him?" she would ask. I paused before answering, only because I wanted her to know I realized how important the answer was to her.

"Yes," I said firmly.

She nodded her consent. "Okay. Kill that bastard."

It was my connection to Ireland that kept me grounded while I stalked Kevin. Although my mind was primarily on Peter and vengeance, my feelings for the Irish people started to grow during that time. It was 1969. The civil rights movement in Ireland had taken root a year earlier, when the Northern Ireland Civil Rights Association (NICRA) had organized street demonstrations to air long-held Catholic grievances against the Unionist government. Southie had had a strong Northern Aid support group for some time, but I'd never been involved. I cannot say for sure why I shifted my attention to Ireland. Somehow Peter's death helped me look at things differently. Maybe my newborn anger transferred to the British. Also, it was something that I could talk about openly with my parents, something other than Peter's death. I remember the sense of justice I felt when I began to raise money for Ireland's cause.

And I had another fight on my hands. In July, while I was devoting much of my energy to the hunt, a gang war erupted between the Killeens and the Mullens. More on that in a minute.

Enough for now to write that I had three irons in the fire: my people's fight overseas, an escalating gang war at home, and the pursuit and destruction of Kevin Daley.

Hunting is an art. There are two phases to hunting: passive and active. Passive hunting is when you watch every step your enemy makes. You watch for weeks, you note everything he does — from what time he leaves for work in the morning to what time he takes out the garbage cans on trash day. You write down every quirk — the shortcuts he takes off Broadway, who he takes to church; you time how long it takes for him to park his car and walk up the front stairs to his house. This is the "homework" phase. The Marine Corps had taught me how to get as close to your enemy as possible without being detected, and how to find and then exploit their weaknesses. I took my jungle warfare training and simply applied it to the streets. It was different, of course, but really only small adjustments were necessary. On the streets your enemy's most vulnerable position is the watering hole: everyone has a place he likes to go, to relax and shoot the shit while drinking a few beers.

After you've gathered enough details, enough to make you sick and stock full of hatred — you make a plan. The execution of that plan is the active hunt — the day of reckoning. Kevin was alive and every time I saw him move I saw Peter lying lifeless on a slab. All I wanted was pure revenge — nothing more.

I'm not sure how much time had passed since Peter's funeral, but one day I felt it was time to act. Paulie McGonagle and I put together a hunt after driving around Southie for hours. We waited for Kevin in a recently stolen four-door Ford outside his favorite bar, Hoolihans, on the corner of H and Eighth. We parked on the corner across the street. Paulie was in the driver's seat and I was squatted low in the back. My weapon of choice back then was a sawed-off shotgun. It was devastating at close range; both barrels were loaded with deer slugs. I'd laid it on the floor next to my mask.

Paulie and I didn't talk much; the anxiety was as thick as a fog. I kept seeing Peter with the two small star-shaped holes over and under his eye; I saw him running with the football on the beach at Castle Island; I saw him sitting at the table drinking coffee with my mother. He'd been home from Vietnam just two months before he was killed. There was irony in the fact that Kevin Daley was also a Vietnam marine.

I thought about killing: the butterflies floated and kicked at the inside of my lower stomach. But I knew I could do it. I had no choice. From the night I saw Peter in the morgue there was never a question that I would not avenge his death. I was obsessed with making Kevin pay.

Kevin staggered out the front door of the bar stone drunk.

"Go!" I said calmly.

I pulled the mask over my face with my right hand while I reached for the shotgun with my left, almost in one motion. The engine fired and Paulie put the transmission in gear. Everything slowed. I pressed the shotgun butt snug into my shoulder. My fingers forced themselves flat against the shiny brown wood. Hatred, rage, and pain held me stiff and I clenched my teeth as I watched my target walk to his car. Kevin grinned to himself. I pictured the exact center of his left temple that I'd blow away.

Crash.

"What the fuck are you doing?" I whispered at Paulie.

Crunch.

"Back up!" I begged.

Paulie was so nervous that he shifted into drive instead of reverse and stomped on the gas pedal. The Ford rocketed forward; the front right wheel smashed the curb and propelled the car into the foundation of the house on the corner.

"Paulie, get out of here quick," I said.

I watched Kevin get into his car and drive away. He never even looked in our direction. But other people, naturally, began to look. Paulie pulled off the curb and sped off. I had to laugh. Shit, how could you get mad at Paulie; he just kept shaking his head. We were thieves, not killers, and at least he had the balls to drive. But I couldn't let Kevin live another month. The weight of it haunted every waking moment. I needed to make that half-inch squeeze of the trigger.

Two weeks later I got another chance. It was a Sunday afternoon; Kevin was playing football with the semiprofessional team known then as the Chippewas at Columbia Park in Southie. The boys and me watched him through binoculars. Kevin had a green Volkswagen Beetle. Donnie spotted it parked along the edge of the street.

Right before the game was about to end, I sent one of the Mullens, Buddy Flynn, to puncture one of Kevin's tires. We were geared up. I had my sawed-off shotgun loaded with deer slug, and this time I wouldn't fail.

The game ended and we watched as the boys shook hands in the middle of the field.

"Paulie," I said, "the *D* on the shift stands for *drive*. Now let's go congratulate Kevin on the win."

I planned to give Kevin a few minutes to get the jack out of his trunk and start raising the car. We figured he'd be engrossed in fixing the tire, either on his knees or bending over. I pulled my mask over my face and lay down. The hum of the engine made me warm inside.

I focused on my next move. Paulie would stop. I would sit up, kick open the door, wait until Kevin turned, give him a second to understand his life was over, smile at him, squeeze the trigger, and destroy his face with both barrels.

"Shit, he's gone," Paulie yelled.

I sat up and whipped off my mask. I laid the shotgun on the floor and stepped out of the car. Buddy had flattened the tire alright. But he'd gotten a little carried away and stuck the knife into two tires. Now what's the chance of getting a flat in two tires on a Sunday afternoon while you play football? Kevin must have come to his car, saw the tires, smelled the ambush, and knew it was time to beat it. But shit, how could you get mad? Buddy had done what I'd asked him to do; he'd just gotten a little too excited about the task. I don't think any of my fellow hunters really understood the full extent of what they were about to do. You had to take our inexperience into account. But I had patience — I knew I'd get Kevin eventually.

It was November 10, 1969, the 194th anniversary of the founding of the Marine Corps — the day every Marine reflects on what it means to be a Marine and the day Marines remember each battle, each courageous feat of combat. Despite the fact that Kevin was a Marine, there was no stopping me. I was going to get him on our birthday.

Some of the Mullens were already watching Kevin's family's house, at M and Third streets. Bobby was in an alley across the street, shotgun filled with birdshot. I lay in the alley behind Kevin's house, dressed head to toe in solid black. It was two o'clock in the morning and it was raining hard, which was in my favor: the rain would cover the sound of my approach, a tactic I'd learned in Vietnam. The houses on Kevin's block were only fifteen feet apart from one another, and I wondered if somebody would see me lying there on the ground. But I figured that both the darkness and my black clothing would camouflage me.

Kevin had a couple of brothers who were Boston police officers. If the brothers heard anything and came out the front door, Bobby would unload the birdshot on them, driving them back into the house. The birdshot wouldn't kill them, just wound. You can't just kill for the sake of killing — there has to be a good reason. Peter's death and Ma and Dad's grief were three good reasons for killing Kevin. But killing a Boston police officer was never an option. You just don't do it.

The rain was running down my cheeks and into my mouth; I tasted the drops in the back of my throat. I'll never forget the aroma of fresh rainfall inside my nostrils. Suddenly I heard the unmistakable rumble of Kevin's old Volkswagen Bug, which needed a muffler job. My stomach jumped. The switch inside my brain turned on.

"This is for you Peter," I whispered.

The vibrating muffler was my call to action. I ran down the alley and crouched low. Kevin had parked directly in front of his house. I was only three feet away. I watched the rain dance off the street in front of his car, and then each and every sound in the world shut off when his engine died. I never heard his door open or his feet scuff on the pavement. I don't remember standing up or moving into the street.

Kevin turned and headed for his front door.

"Hey asshole."

He stopped and turned slowly. I never pulled my mask over my face; I wanted him to see Peter's face in my eyes.

I smiled when he understood what was happening.

"It's your turn."

When he realized he was going to die, his jaw sunk into his chest. I remember wondering if Peter's eyes had had the same look of fear. I raised my .38 automatic and took a shooter's stance: my feet spread to shoulder's width; I crunched down just slightly. I was jacked. He froze at first and then tried to run.

I squeezed.

Twice.

The half-inch squeeze was easy. Both hits ripped tiny holes into his leather jacket. He spun around and bounced off the side of another car parked in the street before his body hit the pavement. I walked slowly over to him. With no hesitation, I squeezed out two more shots, one above the heart and one below. His midsection drilled to the pavement with the impact of the bullets. I kicked him in the face; I can still hear Kevin's teeth shattering on the end of my boot.

"How does it feel, motherfucker?"

I turned to run, but I heard my mother's keening the night Peter died. I couldn't help but feel Peter in that moment. Blood was beginning to gurgle from Kevin's body. I looked down at Kevin and spit.

Nobody came outside; not one light came on. The rain had protected me. Bobby covered me as I backed down the street toward the car. I threw the gun into the backseat and one of the guys immediately started to hacksaw it into pieces. We drove by the ocean and Bobby tossed away the evidence.

"Is he dead?" somebody asked.

"He looked dead to me."

The guys let me off at the Hotel Essex. By this time the Mullens had acquired a master key to every room — one of our guys worked the lobby. Any day or night we just used a room that hadn't been booked. I couldn't go home right away. I wanted to be by myself. What if the police were looking for me? I remember lying there, running through the implications of what I'd just done.

For a split second I wished it all was just a dream: that Peter wasn't dead and that I hadn't just killed Peter's killer. There was no taking back what I'd just done. I'd taken a man's life. I had just looked a man square in the eye and shot four rounds into his body. But I also had no remorse. I knew that what I had just done in some way had set me free. At that moment I didn't care if I went to jail for a long time.

I called Dad from the hotel payphone. He was asleep, but since the night we'd gotten the call about Peter he always answered by the second ring.

"Dad." I paused.

"It's done?"

"He's dead."

"You were home tonight with us," he said.

"Don't worry Dad. I'll be alright."

There was just one small problem: Kevin lived.

Bobby called me the next morning at the hotel and said that Kevin had crawled into a doorway and somebody had gotten him into the hospital in time for him to identify me. All I could think about was spending the next twenty years of my life behind bars. I stopped by my parents to see how they were holding up. My mother was wracked with anguish and thinking she'd lost another son.

I was carrying two guns because I had a hunch somebody might come looking for me. I decided to get out of the house and meet some of the Mullens. As I stepped down the last step of the inside stairwell I saw a Boston police cruiser pull up outside and double park. They hadn't seen me. I ran back upstairs and stashed the guns under the couch. I had to turn myself in. I headed quickly down the stairs, stepped out the front door, and closed it behind me. Now they couldn't go inside to search for anything.

"Pat, we have a warrant for your arrest. You've been charged with attempted murder."

I was held without bail in the old Charles Street Jail near Beacon Hill. Two months later they wheeled Kevin into court to testify against me. He was connected to an IV. I'm not sure why now, but I almost laughed out loud when I saw him.

The prosecutor read Kevin's deathbed declaration. It didn't look good for me. Even my lawyer thought I was sunk for at least twenty. They put Kevin on the stand and that's when my luck turned, almost as if Peter was up there looking after me.

"Can you identify the shooter in the courtroom?" the prosecutor asked.

"Well, now, taking a good look at him, up close and all, I know this is not him," Kevin muttered.

I wanted to explode with relief and exhilaration, but instead I bit down hard on the inside of my lower lip. I couldn't show a hint of cockiness.

The judge was an Irishman who hated us Southie guys. "Are you sure, Mr. Daley?" the judge asked.

"Yes sir. I can't say that this is the man who shot me."

The judge's face turned a shade of dark purple, and he refused to dismiss the case against me. But in the end he had no choice but to free me and send me back to the streets to fight the Killeens.

11. THE SOUTHIE GANG WAR

War is war. It doesn't matter if you're in Vietnam or Southie — war is a game of kill or be killed. Of course, it goes beyond that. I became fascinated with war histories, finding out who won, figuring out what the winning side had done to avoid getting killed and what the other side had done (or not done) to lose. The guys who got killed followed their same old routines; they got complacent, usually because they were arrogant. I was determined to study the example of the winners.

After my acquittal my desire to kill Kevin simply disappeared. Peter was dead, my mother didn't want to lose me to a long jail sentence, and if Kevin wound up dead it's no doubt who the number-one suspect would be. I don't know why, in the end, Kevin refused to identify me. Maybe he realized that he had it coming to him; maybe he was grateful to have lived and knew that if he did rat me out another of the Mullens would get him in the end. In any case, I was back on the street with the Mullens, defending our turf and amassing our skills as criminals.

The shooting war had started seven months earlier, one summer night in July of 1969. Some of the Southie guys from the Killeens and the Mullens — including me — were drinking at The Improper Bostonian, right behind the Roxy in downtown Boston. The Killeen brothers — Donald, Kenneth, and Edward — were big-time organized criminals who ran the sports betting and loan sharking in Southie. The Killeens controlled every illegal activity that emerged in South Boston for nearly two decades. They used muscle to make collections, and to make examples of those deadbeats who didn't pay in a timely fashion.

The Mullens, by contrast, were a loosely organized bunch of

thieves. But being in Southie, it was just a matter of time before we butted heads with the Killeens. I knew it wouldn't be on account of a business conflict, because we had our little niche and they had their own bigger niche. No, I always knew that when it happened it would be because of booze and bad tempers.

I was sitting at the bar next to Whitey Bulger. We knew each other from Southie — that was the extent of our acquaintance. He was forty and I had just turned twenty-five. I remember his biceps bulging out of his extra-tight blue t-shirt as he lifted his beer. Whitey kept buying me drinks and I accepted out of respect. We never mentioned the Killeens or the Mullens. I knew he was muscle for the Killeens and he knew I was a Mullen. We talked about getting laid and other such matters of import in our world. I'll never forget how pretentious Whitey was. He just loved hearing himself talk.

"I'm an expert on military maneuvers, Pat," he said. "I've studied Patton and MacArthur. Read everything I could about strategies of war." I nodded politely, while inside my head I was holding a different conversation with him: "Fuck you, asshole. Anything you know about war comes from a book. You've never actually done shit."

"So you saw combat in Vietnam, I heard."

"Some, not much really. Not like the heavy shit they're facing now."

He kept asking me about Vietnam, but I didn't trust him enough to talk about it. His hairline was receding and a thick gold chain hung from his neck. I couldn't help but notice how his gaze traveled, never resting on one object for more than a few seconds.

Everything changed forever when Mickey Dwyer came stumbling in the front door. Mickey, a senior member of the Mullen gang, was a friend of mine and a pretty fair boxer. Sober, he was barely comprehensible, but now he sounded like a guy with a bad harelip. Whitey and I struggled to understand what he was trying to say. He'd been at the Transit, a bar near Broadway Station in Southie. I guess he'd been running his mouth about the Mullens and Southie. Kenny Killeen, who ran the Killeens with his brother Donnie, thought he was talking out of school and took offense. Kenny Killeen had bitten off Mickey's nose and shot him three times in his right arm.

Whitey and I both sighed; we both knew what this would mean. It was then that I noticed Mickey's face: he was stunned to see Whitey there. Mickey knew who Whitey was to the Killeens — he was one of their most feared enforcers.

"This ain't good." Whitey said.

"Nope," was all I said.

I didn't want to tip my hand to Whitey. If it was going to be war, I didn't want my enemy knowing what was in my head. Somebody told me that Paulie McGonagle and some of the other Mullens were already headed to the Transit to confront Kenny Killeen.

Whitey and I pushed our drinks away and headed for the door together. The place was buzzing. Whitey, I knew, was bound for the Transit. He sensed I was headed there too. You could smell it in the air — a showdown was on the way. We didn't speak as we crossed the street. The energy from the collision of these two gangs sobered me up fast.

"You want to hop a ride?" he asked.

I didn't hesitate. "Sure."

We rode in complete silence; I wondered if we would speak before we parked. There was a spot right in front of the Transit, but Whitey drove past it and parked further up the street. "Clever prick," I thought: he wanted some space to see who was in the Transit, or who might come out, and a short walk would give him that space. I waited and he put out his hand to me.

"Probably won't be talking to you again," he said.

I shook his hand firmly. "No, I guess not."

We reached for our door handles at the same time and walked

down to the Transit together. Just then a few of the Mullens came out of the bar. Whitey and I were still thirty yards or so away. I saw a few of the senior Mullens — Paulie McGonagle, Jimmy Lydon, and Buddy Roache — standing and talking seriously as Whitey and I approached. They looked up in muted surprise. I could read their eyes: "What the fuck is Pat doing with Whitey?"

As I greeted them, Whitey casually walked into the Transit. He was being pretty cool, I thought. Paulie McGonagle, Jimmy Lydon, and Buddy Roache were some of the toughest guys in the Mullens — and in Southie — hand to hand. They weren't known as shooters, just serious with their fists. Whitey showed some courage walking by these genuinely tough men who were highly pissed about what Kenny Killeen, Whitey's boss, had done to one of us. And Whitey, the prick, I've got to hand it to him: he did it with confidence.

As I watched Whitey walk into the Transit I realized I'd probably have to kill him one day. I knew he'd try to kill me. I knew where this was going; I knew the dynamic of what had started, not by experience but by common street sense. And I knew what would be at stake if we challenged the Killeens. And if we won.

I explained to Paulie, Jimmy, and Buddy that I'd been drinking with Whitey when Mickey Dwyer came stumbling into the bar. The guys had come here to set things straight with the Killeens. They wanted to even the score — one of our guys was down. But the Killeens had left the bar, so we walked away to plot our next move.

The fact that these guys were there to take on the Killeens was as ballsy as hell, and they showed guts, but Mickey had been shot! They weren't even bringing a knife to this gunfight! I guess Paulie and the guys thought they could overcome the Killeens' guns with their fists, bottles, or whatever they could get their hands on. I admired that, of course. But the Killeens had Billy O'Sullivan and

Whitey and a few other guys as their enforcers — their killers. At any rate, Paulie, Jimmy, and Buddy had already missed Kenny Killeen and his guys, who'd left before they got there.

We decided to go back into the Transit in case any of the Killeens had slipped in through the back door. Whitey stood alone at one end of the bar. He certainly didn't look scared. I think we stayed for about an hour or so, but the Killeens never returned. I suggested we go home and come up with a plan of action. Before we left Nick "The Greek," who owned the place, smirked at me. I heard later that he told Whitey that the Mullens would all be dead in a month.

What Paulie, Jimmy, and Buddy had done by showing up at the Transit was incite a gang war — a war in which the odds were stacked strongly against us. Us against the Killeens? A pack of thieves against Southie's organized crime? We were goners.

Let me explain.

Given the fact that Kenny Killeen was second only to his big brother, Donald, as Southie's crime boss, his maiming and shooting of Mickey should have simply been accepted, not challenged. "Yeah, that's right, I did it. What are you punks going to do about it?" That was Kenny's unspoken message. Or, to put it in terms citizens can understand: "I'm organized crime, with money and enforcers; you're a bunch of thieves. Accept it or I'll kill you all." By going back to the Transit to look for Kenny, the Mullens showed we weren't going to take it. The Killeens — and all of Southie — knew that the Mullens had gone back to the Transit, and that sealed it. The Killeens now had to respond. They could not ignore even such a seemingly slight challenge to their dominance. They would crush the Mullens for even thinking about it: that's how it works. The Mafia, Hell's Angels, the Bloods, the Crips, the Russian mobs: every gang operates from this same dynamic.

I was all for revenge: Kenny shot and maimed one of us. Hey, we can shoot too. I wasn't scared of them. I had successfully hunted prey in Vietnam, and I believed I had the skills to help the Mullens win against the Killeens. I wasn't planning on losing.

Billy O'Sullivan, or Billy O', muscle for the Killeen gang, was a Southie marine just like me. Marines always give fellow marines respect and special consideration. Sure, sometimes you find out that the guy you're trying to help is an asshole, but the Marine Corps instills in you a code of brotherhood that comes to the fore in every first interaction with a fellow marine.

Billy O'Sullivan was thin with piercing steel-blue eyes. He was a veteran of the Charlestown gang war of the early 1960s, which left many dead on both sides. He was fearless. Everybody loved to party with Billy; his wit and charm could be hypnotic. But he was also mean and volatile; he'd shoot you in the eye for a perceived insult. He simply refused to stand for any disrespect whatsoever.

After Billy O', Whitey was the Killeen's second most-feared enforcer. In the late 1950s and early 1960s Whitey had done time in Alcatraz and Leavenworth prisons, among others, for robbing banks. He had come back to Southie in 1965 after getting out on parole. Back then nobody really knew too much about Whitey, except that he was an egomaniac and in fierce physical shape.

Now the Mullens were knee deep in shit. We had no experience in gang warfare. We couldn't match the manpower of the Killeens. We had some tough guys, no doubt, but beating guys with your fists or with a baseball bat is one thing; it's another to use guns. It takes a certain type of personality to squeeze a round into a man's chest or head and watch his tissue explode in front of your face. Not many guys have that ability. You take everything from a man when you kill him. There's no taking it back. You face life in jail and revenge from his family or friends. It's deadly serious business. All the shooters I've ever known had an uncanny ability to detach themselves from their victims and from the act.

There is no such thing as a heroic hit man; there is no good in taking a man's life. But this situation had been thrust on the Mullens, so becoming shooters now became a matter of survival.

About a week or so later, with no warning, Billy O' dropped by to see me at old Dorgan's Pub on the corner of G and Marine Streets. He came by himself, which showed respect. His eyes twinkled with mischief. I guess he thought we had a lot in common. We were both from Southie, both marines and criminals. I'd seen combat in Vietnam, and I'd heard that Billy saw some serious shit in Korea.

I was tense and ready when I saw Billy come in — I was packing my Colt 1911, a .45 caliber, one of my favorite weapons. I looked around for Whitey, but he wasn't in sight. "He may be nearby," I thought. Billy greeted me warmly and we sat at the end of the bar. We ordered a few beers. I pushed my bicep against my holstered .45, inside my jacket, for reassurance. I was ready for anything. While I appeared calm and friendly, I was going through all the "what if" scenarios: What if he draws on me right away? What if he goes to the bathroom and comes out shooting? What if Whitey comes rushing in the back door?

"Pat, you shouldn't be involved with these people," he said. "You're a good kid and I wouldn't want to see you get hurt."

"I gotta stay with them, Billy," I said. "They're my friends."

"Why don't you just get away from all this? It's going to get ugly for them."

"Sorry, Billy, I could never do that."

I respected Billy. He was a veteran and a killer. I knew what made him tick. I watched him walk out the front door. I wasn't backing down. The situation had come to a point where shooting was inevitable. So I began to consider how to get them before they got me.

———

I can't remember how long it took for the shooting to begin, but it started one night when Billy O' and Whitey confronted Buddy Roache in a bar on Broadway. I don't think Billy and Whitey expected to find Buddy there; if they had anticipated that they would have ambushed him outside. Buddy and Billy O', both with huge egos, found themselves in the middle of a heated argument. Billy O' pulled out a .22 and shot Buddy in the left shoulder; the bullet exited near his spine. A .22 caliber is a small round but it's really fast. The slug does crazy things inside the human body; it jumps and skips around, destroying everything in its path. The trauma caused damage to Buddy's spine — he never walked again.

Then Donnie McGonagle, Paulie's brother, was gunned down dead. The word on the street was that it was Billy O' and Whitey, which made sense. Donnie was not involved with the Mullen gang, but he was Paulie's double — Billy O' thought he was killing Paulie but instead he got Donnie, a noncombatant. I'm sure Billy didn't shed a goddamn tear over his mistake.

The Mullens arranged a meeting at the Hotel Essex. We had to attack. Paulie stepped up and volunteered to take charge. He had to stop Billy O', but Paulie wanted more — he wanted to avenge his brother. If he could take out Billy O' he'd deal a severe blow to the Killeens. The Mullens would be taking out the Killeen's deadliest guy, and the psychological impact of that would severely shake their confidence.

Paulie had to find out where Billy O' lived, hung out, and so on. Which he did. The rest of this story is only what I've been told. Paulie gave me all these details. I have no idea if it's bullshit, but the end result wasn't.

He said it was a Sunday, about midnight. Billy O' had just gotten out of his car up on Savin Hill near his house. He'd been at Kelly's Cork & Bull for a party for his cousin. I guess he was a little drunk, staggering slightly and whistling.

The act was simple, but the planning behind it had taken time and patience. Paulie had been there for hours. He sat at the crest of the hill behind some shrubs. He was dressed entirely in black and his face was covered by a deep-blue ski mask. There were no lights at the crest, just a patch of dark gray. It was a perfect shield.

Billy walked by the shrubs. Paulie jumped up and aimed his .45 at the middle of Billy's back. Paulie told me he wasn't the slightest bit frightened. Billy heard the sound of the .45 cocking in the night air. He spun around and his eyes registered what the arrogant prick never could have conceived: someone had the drop on him.

"Shit! I'm dead," Billy gasped.

"You're right," Paulie growled.

Paulie didn't hesitate. Pulling the trigger on Billy O' was easy. After all — Billy had killed Donnie, Paulie's brother. I guess Billy crumpled pretty hard on the pavement but never for an instant showed any fear. When I heard about it the next day I felt a tinge of remorse. We were all just Southie guys. But then Paulie reminded me that this was war — and Billy O' and Whitey had killed his brother Donnie.

For the next several weeks the streets were pretty quiet — tense, but quiet. The Boston police had their organized crime unit out in full force. Rumors ran wild around Boston about the identity of the shooter. The North End mafia, the Irish Winter Hill gang: nobody could believe Billy O' had been gunned down. The Killeens weren't so confident anymore. Now the weight of their muscle fell on the shoulders of Whitey Bulger.

One night I was walking to the Hotel Essex with my Smith & Wesson snub-nosed .38 tucked inside the pocket of my warm-up jacket. It was a light windbreaker, and the weight of the gun really forced the pocket open. It was a pain in the ass to keep it from falling out, but I'd left the apartment I was staying in — I'd moved out of my Southie home for the duration of the war — in a real hurry. Just as I was entering the Essex an unmarked cruiser pulled up next to me. The guy inside was a Boston police detective and a real evil fucker; he made Harvey Keitel in *Bad Lieutenant* look like a Peace Corps volunteer. This guy was simply a gangster with a badge.

"Get in the car," Welsh ordered.

I thought about running and ditching the gun. He might have caught me but never would have got the gun. I'd never shoot a cop, even this prick; it just wasn't an option. But I decided to bluff him instead. I opened the back door and slid in.

"What's going on?" I joked.

"I like you Pat. You know that," he said.

He hated me. And he thought I was stupid enough to believe him.

"Listen, we just heard Red was going to plant a bomb in your car. He was spotted in your driveway. Pat, I don't want you to get hurt. I thought you should know."

Red was a Killeen.

Suddenly I could feel the .38 starting to slide out of my pocket. It's a compact pistol, but well made with some good heft to it. And my pocket was worn and ripped from the weight of the guns I carried. I couldn't put my hand in my pocket because Welsh would spot the motion and tell me to pull out whatever I had in there. I couldn't move. The angle at which I was sitting had caused the pocket to open and the pistol's barrel was now protruding a good inch out of a tear in the pocket. If I even took a breath my gun would snake out and bounce off the floor mat. If that happened and it didn't make too much noise, I planned on toeing it slowly under the front seat and then getting the hell out of there.

"Thanks for telling me. I really appreciate it."

I squeezed my elbow tightly against my side to keep the gun from falling as I reached for the door handle with my other hand. It was just pure luck; the tip of my elbow caught the gun's handle. I never expected my gun to make the climb out of the backseat. For sure the .38 would bounce off the pavement. But I lucked out.

I waved as he sped away, no doubt laughing to himself. But I had the last laugh: not only did he fail to get me on a gun charge, he hadn't succeeded in fooling me — I didn't even own a car for Red to plant a bomb in. He was just trying to stir the pot. He must have been confident that I'd go immediately and grab Red outside the Coachman, his favorite barroom. I bet the detectives sat there all night waiting for me.

In war you have to calculate and anticipate your enemy's next move so you can organize a counterambush. For weeks the Mullen gang prepared for a full-scale attack by the Killeens. We moved out of our homes, altered our social habits, slept in the day and hunted at night. None of us held full-time jobs; our full-time commitment was to watching the enemy, gathering intelligence, and readying ourselves for Whitey's attack. We also gathered our arsenal of guns and ammo, cleaned the guns, and situated our boilers in garages around the city.

Paulie and Jimmy stored weapons all over Southie, Charlestown, and Somerville. The Mullens stole cars with registrations and keys; we had several friends at a fancy Boston hotel who worked as valets and who would call us whenever a late model midsize four-door was available. We'd change the plates and park the cars in friendly garages throughout the city. Each trunk held a camouflaged duffel bag stocked with gloves and an array of guns (usually a 30.06 rifle, two pistols, and a shotgun), ski masks, wigs, and a gallon container filled with gas. The 30.06 was meant for shooting out the engine block of a police cruiser if any of us were being chased. Paulie and Jimmy had strategically placed each of our cars around Southie, within blocks of one another.

The Mullens were ready. At least a dozen active members had a role. We set about trying to track every move made by the Killeen brothers and Whitey Bulger. The Mullens had loyalists all over Southie. One called in Whitey's positions; another let Jimmy know where Donald Killeen was from 9 P.M. to midnight every night. They were determined not to allow the prediction on the streets — that the Mullens wouldn't last a month — to come true. Whitey and the Killeens had definitely misjudged our abilities. Still, it was challenging and time-consuming to get guys right where the Mullens wanted them: in their gunsights. Because we had to avoid getting caught by the police, too.

One confrontation came in the middle of rush hour. I was sitting in Mallows Tavern near South Station with Paulie. The sun was glaring through the plate glass windows. We'd positioned ourselves so that we could see cars and people passing by. Outside the Boston traffic idled. I looked up and saw a blue four-door Ford LTD roughly forty yards away.

"Shit, it's Whitey," I said to Paulie.

"What are you gonna do?"

"He's trapped. I got him."

"Pat, there are too many people outside and it's fucking rush hour, for Christ's sake!"

"Give me your gun."

Paulie slid me his .32 under the table and I put it in my jacket pocket. Once outside, I started running toward Whitey's car. As I got closer I recognized Jack Curran, one of the Killeen enforcers, in the backseat. By now I had the pistol out. I remember running by citizens sitting in their cars with their mouths wide open. Pedestrians on the sidewalk parted like the Red Sea. I was twenty yards away and closing on the car. I hopped into the street, my arms pumping as I picked up the pace; I was dodging people and cars the whole distance. The thought of getting caught and going to jail occurred to me, but only briefly: I figured it was better than getting killed by Whitey or another of the Killeens. Plus, if Whitey had seen me first, he wouldn't even think of not killing me. You've got to seize the opportunity when it comes. I'd waited a long time for this.

The guy I knew as Red was sitting in the back of the car with Jack Curran; he was the first to spot me. They were sitting ducks — two cars had locked them in at a red light, one car in front of them and the other behind. I remember Whitey turning and making eye contact. He wasn't scared. His eyes had the same calculating gaze I'd seen the night we sat together at the Improper Bostonian — before the war began.

Whitey pulled up onto the median strip with two tires. Then he edged past the two cars forcing him to wait for the red light. The Ford's underbelly scraped off the cement; sparks flew. Horns blared. I was thirty, maybe twenty feet from their car. I had to do something quickly — Whitey was getting away. I heard sirens off in the distance; I knew they weren't for me, it was too soon. I was quickly figuring out when I'd stop and start shooting. I expected them to be armed, so in a flash I looked around for a spot to use as cover, maybe a bench or a mailbox. I raised my gun, stopped running, and steadied my aim. But I have to give it to Whitey: he was a hell of a driver. By the time I had a clear shot he was just too far away, and the field of fire was crowded with innocent citizens.

I missed Whitey that time, but two things had been established: Whitey now knew I was the one actively hunting him, and I knew that he was vulnerable during the day — he was on the street unarmed. That must have been so, because they certainly would have opened fire on me if they had been armed. Any cop spotting Whitey, Jack, and Red cruising around during the day could pull them over, and if they had guns, it'd be off to jail with them. I realized, too, that Whitey would now be looking to get me before any other Mullen.

Shortly afterward, Jimmy and I took to the streets of Whitey's neighborhood. I put on a long dark wig and a mustache and Jimmy slipped into one of his girlfriend's dresses and a blond wig. I borrowed my friend's daughter's favorite doll and a baby's car seat and we headed out for a family drive. We had Donald Killeen in our sights many times, but the bastard was smart. He never went anywhere during the day without his ten-year-old son at his side. In Southie there were rules, and one of them was that you never killed around a child. We were criminals, but we weren't animals. We had a code of conduct and if you violated it, you'd find your-self alone — or dead.

By this point I had moved out of Southie and into Charlestown. It just wasn't safe to be around my family during a shooting war. My girlfriend, Ronnie, had a place at 106 Walford Way in the Bunker Hill housing projects. Nobody knew I was there. I had a fail-safe way of doubling back on myself every time I left Southie; that way I could see if Whitey was tailing me. Ronnie had a daughter, Theresa, and a son, Jimmy, from a previous marriage. On April 23, 1971, Ronnie gave birth to our son, Patrick Nee, Jr. I'm not going to talk much about Ronnie or Patrick. I refuse to make their lives a part of my criminal history.

One night the Mullens needed to get a message to me. Jerry Roake came to see me in Charlestown after he'd had too many beers. The instant I saw him at the door I was apprehensive.

"Jerry, did anybody follow you?"

"No, I watched my mirror and I drove around the block three times. Nobody followed me. I made sure of it, Pat."

Two nights later I was sitting watching television in Ronnie's first-floor apartment. My .45 was on the coffee table next to me, covered by a dishtowel. Theresa was sitting in front of me on the floor playing with Legos. Ronnie was in the kitchen cleaning up after supper. I was tired from hunting Whitey and was planning on going to bed early.

It was then that I noticed a rifle barrel reflected in the window. I saw Whitey in the corner of the window; he was looking right

Pat's mother Julia, left, poses with the Judes, her family clan.

Pat's father, Patrick, third from right, stands with the Paddas, his family clan.

Scoil Rosmúc, Pat's one-room schoolhouse in Rosmuc. Pat stands in top row, third from left. Peter sits on his right hand in the middle of the first row. Both are wearing sweaters knit by their mother.

A Nee family photo taken in 1957 at Ciro's Studio on Bowdoin Street in Dorchester, Massachusetts. Pat sits holding his sisters, Barbara and Mary, as Michael, Sean, and Peter stand left to right.

Pat, on the left, stands in front of his family home on East Third Street in South Boston with young Mullens in 1960. Jerry Yarnovitch is furthest right; Jerry Shea stands next to him. Pat's mother and sisters are looking out the window.

Seventeen-year-old Pat, the day he graduated from Parris Island and became a United States Marine.

Pat takes a break with fellow marines in 1963 on maneuvers in the Mediterranean.

Pat celebrates with mother Julia in 1966 on his first Christmas home after leaving the Marine Corps.

Peter Nee

Peter drinks a beer with a pilot during his tour in Vietnam.

Whitey Bulger, sitting at right, celebrates the wedding of a friend with Pat Nee and his wife, Debbie.

Bob Andersen, photographed in 2005.

Sue and Joe Murray together in 1984. Their relationship ended violently and abruptly; Sue shot Joe several times during a domestic argument.

The *Valhalla* being secured by investigators in Boston Harbor on October 16, 1984. *Photo credit: Boston Herald*

The *Marita Ann*, now named the *Daragh Liam*, docked at Howth, Ireland.

Pat stands on the cliffs overlooking Galway Bay the day before seven tons of weapons were seized from the *Marita Ann*.

at me. I lunged for my .45, threw the magazine into it, and pulled the slide back. Whitey took aim. Theresa saw me grab the gun. She stood up, confused. Theresa was right in the field of fire. Everything stopped. I glanced at Whitey. For seconds nobody moved. Then Whitey lowered the gun barrel, smiled, and took off running. I picked up Theresa, ran to the bedroom, threw her softly onto the bed, and grabbed my 30.06 rifle from the closet.

The bedroom window faced north, the same direction in which Whitey had escaped. I opened the window and jumped to the pavement. There must have been a dozen residents walking or sitting on their stoops. But it didn't matter, this was Charlestown — nobody saw a thing.

I picked up Whitey in a full run in the middle of the housing project courtyard. He was dressed in dungarees and a tight black t-shirt; his rifle moved by his side. I dropped to my knees in the middle of the courtyard, inhaled, and focused into my scope. Whitey had just turned a corner toward a small parking lot. I saw a car door open. I was seventy feet from him, locked into position and waiting for a clear shot. The crosshair in my scope jumped from trees to benches to cars. I couldn't get a clear shot at the back of his head, although a chest shot would have done the trick. But then Whitey was in the car and the squealing of the tires echoed off the project walls. I stood up and walked slowly back to the apartment.

"Hey Pat, " somebody chuckled.

I just waved at the air. The bastard had caught another break. But he had my respect for not taking his shot when Theresa was in the crossfire.

After that Whitey hit me twice. The first time Jimmy Mantville and I were double-parked on M Street, waiting to talk to a friend. I was in the driver's seat and wasn't watching the mirror. "Duck," Jimmy yelled suddenly. Three shooters in black ski masks suddenly pulled up beside us. The shooter in the passenger's seat wielded a sawed-off shotgun. Whitey was driving; I would have recognized those eyes anywhere, even behind a ski mask. The other shooter was in the backseat pointing his .38 in our direction.

Flashes of light and flying glass surrounded us almost instantly. Within seconds Jimmy was crawling out the passenger-side door and I rolled out from behind the steering wheel.

I'm not sure why — rage, I guess — but I took off running after Whitey's car. I didn't even have a gun on me — I had nothing for my own protection. I was chasing after his car screaming, "Come back, you motherfucker," when Whitey saw me. He locked up the brakes and pulled a quick U-turn. "Now I'm dead," I thought. I didn't even have something to throw at the car. All of a sudden I saw an alley on my right and dove into it. It's a good thing Whitey kept driving, because I was wide open there on the cement.

They missed us that day but they killed our car. The driver's side was riddled with something like forty bullet holes. The shotgun blasts had demolished every piece of glass and blown away a chunk of the roof. When the Boston police arrived, guns drawn, they couldn't believe we were still alive. A young, green detective took us to Station 6 on D Street and Broadway and questioned us, but neither one of us could remember much. I was just thankful Whitey and his boys couldn't shoot straight.

A week later a dozen or so of us were hanging on the corner of O and Third, getting ready to go Whitey hunting. It was dusk on an early summer evening. In Vietnam we always moved at dusk, because the shadows changed depth and played tricks with your perception. Across the street was a vacant lot, overgrown with weeds. You could see Third Street pretty clearly from our view.

"Hey, look who's in that parked car," Harry the Hat piped up. "It's fucking Whitey!"

"Let's go get them!" Jerry moved toward his trunk for the guns.

It just didn't look right. The way they lounged so nonchalantly

— they wanted us to see them. It was just too obvious. I'd had a nose for this stuff since Vietnam. It was an ambush, no doubt.

"Don't go, Harry, it's a setup," I warned.

"Pat, look at them! They're in our neighborhood and they're flaunting it!" Jerry said, "We gotta go get them."

"I'm not going. Believe me, they're setting an ambush."

Harry, Buddy Leonard, and Jerry went anyway. Jerry turned onto Third Street near M Street Park; their car passed out of sight. Seconds later we heard an M16 open up. By the time we got there to help, Jerry's arm had been blown away. All the tissue from the elbow down was splattered on the car's upholstery. Harry was lying down across the backseat. Buddy had managed to jump out of the car. Neither had been hit. The ambulance rushed Jerry to Massachusetts General Hospital. The doctors cut Jerry's stomach open and sewed his arm to his stomach. I guess that was the only way to save his arm. The rest of us took off before the cops got there.

After a year "in the trenches" the gang war was getting to be a real hassle. The police would hold us for hours asking stupid questions about Whitey Bulger, even though they knew we weren't going to answer them. After Whitey's two failed attempts to end my life and the lives of other Mullens, I was beginning to seriously doubt his abilities. I remember thinking "We've got this guy." It was just a matter of time before we nailed him.

It was really Jimmy Mantville who ended the war for the Mullens. Some people say that he made up his story about taking down Donnie Killeen, that somebody else did it. In fact, there was a rumor going around that Whitey shot his own boss, but that was a story Whitey could have started to elevate his own stature. You don't shoot your boss in the middle of a gang war.

I believed Jimmy. He just wanted to end it all and he figured taking down Donnie Killeen would begin that process. I know the *Boston Globe* and police reports may have a different account of what happened, but this is what Jimmy told me.

Jimmy said he got Donald Killeen outside his house in the Boston suburb of Framingham. It was May 13, 1972. One of our loyal friends had called Jimmy at a bar and given him Donald's address. Jimmy couldn't find anyone but Tommy King to go with him, so they decided to scout the place themselves. He wasn't going there to shoot Donald; his intention was only to gather intelligence. But things just happened.

Donald lived in a new development, with trees on one side of the house and trees in the back. Jimmy sat at the edge of the tree line all night. Donald came home and parked his New Yorker in the driveway, about thirty feet from Jimmy's location. A cement-lined overflow basin started near the tree line and passed within ten feet of Donald's car before it ran under the street. The grade from the end of the driveway was even for about five feet before it sloped down quite sharply to meet the overflow basin. It provided excellent cover — Jimmy said there was no way Donald could see him from the house. He'd lucked out; he couldn't have been given a better location for an ambush.

When Jimmy saw the lights come on in the house at daybreak, he didn't even give it a second thought. He told me it just seemed natural — he made his move. Jimmy and Tommy crawled into the water basin, guns in hand. Their plan was to wait until they heard Donald's car door open and close.

Donald opened and closed his car door for the last time around 6:15 A.M. Jimmy and Tommy sprang from the basin and moved quickly for a headshot. Jimmy told me Donald saw him and went for the glove box. He must have been reaching for a weapon. Jimmy and Tommy fired from five feet away. The first shot hit Donald's shoulder and spun him sideways in the seat. You've got to give that tough prick credit, though. Donald didn't freeze. He kept moving toward the glove box.

But he never got there. Donald looked up and Jimmy and Tommy shot him eight times in the head and neck, right through the window; the flash of blood sprayed the window like paint. Then they ran through the trees back to their car. They threw the guns in the ocean crossing the bridge back into Southie and drove home for a shower.

The war was over. Whitey Bulger, Kenny Killeen, and the rest of the Killeen gang went into hiding. The Mullens celebrated for days. I remember walking into the Transit and seeing Nick the Greek behind the bar smoking a fat cigar. When he saw me his olive skin turned gray. There were twelve or thirteen of us; I didn't have to say anything to him about his earlier prediction that we wouldn't last. We all ate steak tips and drank beers, and then I approached the bar.

"Nick."

His knees buckled under the fat hanging over his belt.

"Pat, how are you? How was the food?" he asked.

Right then a group of six construction workers entered the front door.

"Hey guys, come on in," I said, "sit down and eat. The steak tips are fantastic. Everything you, my friends, and I eat or drink today is on Nick here."

Not a muscle in Nick's face moved.

"You don't have any problems with that, do you Nick?" I asked.

"No, no, that's fine, Pat."

"In fact guys, it's on Nick every day you come in here for lunch or supper."

Nobody laughed. Nobody cheered. Nobody reacted at all. And Nick understood just how much he had underestimated the Mullens.

12. "THE TRUCE"

For the next few weeks the atmosphere at the Mullens' corner was pure elation. The buzz around town had us going for Whitey next. But Whitey went underground — nobody knew where he was hiding. I had a hunch he might be holed up at a friend's down on Cape Cod.

Everybody thought we'd take over Southie, but I had a gut feeling we should end it. I can't tell you what changed my thinking. I just remember waking up and thinking to myself that the killing had to stop.

I sat on it for a few days before I finally went to Tommy King and Jimmy Mantville. After all, they were the ones who had given us dominance by assassinating Donald in his driveway. I thought it right I go to them first.

I wasn't sure how well it would go over. Most of the guys' egos were off the charts; naturally the gang members who talked the loudest weren't the ones doing the shooting. In fact, they hadn't even pointed a gun at anyone, but they wanted the war to go on. Hell, why wouldn't they? They weren't putting themselves in the line of fire; it didn't cost them a thing. Still, I assumed it would be a hard sell to get them to put down our guns and end it.

"Let's get Whitey first," Tommy reasoned.

"No, it's over. Besides, he might get one of us before we get him," I replied.

"Yeah, but if we let him live he'll get us someplace down the road," Jimmy jumped in.

"Not if we put ourselves in the right position — with the right people," I firmly stated. Tommy didn't quite understand what I was trying to say. I could count on the guy's loyalty — he was dangerous, and he was a shooter, but he wasn't one of the sharpest members of the Mullens.

I knew that we had earned capital on the streets by showing our own brand of muscle.

The next week I brought Tommy to Somerville to see Howie Winter, leader of Somerville's powerful Winter Hill gang. (The gang wasn't named for Howie; their headquarters were on Winter Hill in Somerville.) I'd done business with Howie in the past. I didn't need a preset meeting; in fact, I never had to tell him I was coming. Howie was a gentleman, a straight shooter, and he had taken a liking to me.

We found Howie at Joe MacDonald's house, down the street from Pal Joe's Nightclub. There was a bar in the back room where Howie usually hung out. I knocked on the door and Joe led me to the kitchen for coffee. Howie was dressed, as usual, like a blue-collar guy who was doing pretty well. No airs or pretenses for Howie. Joe MacDonald was Howie's best friend. He was Irish and very dangerous.

We shook hands and exchanged the usual pleasantries. Finally, I got to the point.

"Howie, I'd like to end this shooting. Can you help make a truce?"

Howie laughed.

"Who is this guy Whitey?" he snickered.

"He's a Southie guy, a bank robber, did some time in Alcatraz. Him and Billy O' were the Killeen's main muscle."

"Pat, I just got a call from Gerry Angiulo," his voice cracked again with laughter. "Ten minutes ago. He told me Joe Russo called him this morning about you."

"Really?" I said, surprised. Joe was a stand-up guy, a made Mafia lieutenant. I always liked Joe; he was always good to me. Joe owned a nightclub in East Boston.

"Gerry told me Whitey came in last night and begged him for

help. He's been hiding at Hank Garrity's place down on the Cape. He told Joe he didn't think he'd survive Nee."

Sometimes life just plays out that way. You get lucky, and this time I was: Whitey was scared. I've stayed alive a long time by being honest with myself and trusting my instincts.

Tommy thought for sure Howie would tell us we should kill Whitey, that he would talk me out of making a truce. But Howie had never heard of Whitey before the phone call from Joe Russo. Once he came back from Alcatraz and Leavenworth, Whitey rarely crossed the bridges out of Southie for any criminal activity. He couldn't, because Howie and Gerry controlled it all.

Howie called Gerry. A meeting was set for the following Sunday morning at ten at Chandler's Restaurant on Columbus Avenue in Boston's South End. Howie spoke for me and Joe Russo spoke for Whitey. There would be no treachery — no weapons would show up at this meeting. You didn't cross those two guys. Gennaro "Gerry" Angiulo ran the Boston mafia for Raymond Patriarca, who was based in Providence, and Howie's Winter Hill gang was the most powerful non-Mafia gang in New England. The bottom line was that these were deadly guys with lots of guns. No one would act counter to their intentions for this meeting.

I got up at six that morning. It was late fall and the leaves covered the grass at M Street Park; all the trees were barren. It was one of those mornings when you can taste winter directly over your shoulder. Chandler's was owned by two brothers, Jimmy and Johnny Martorano, both stand-up (and dangerous) Winter Hill guys; Johnny already had a number of kills under his belt and was known for his no-nonsense attitude. The plan was that Tommy and I would go into Chandler's and the other Mullens would wait around the corner. If we didn't come out, their job was to come in shooting. Of course, first we had to stake out the place. I think we got there around eight, just to see if Whitey and Kenny Killeen had had the same idea.

"Pat, I don't feel good about this," Tommy spoke out.

"It's gonna be okay. You're just saying that cause you'd like to kill Whitey," I responded.

"No, believe me, Pat. Whitey's not one of us. You have to trust your partners. I'll say it again: This will come back to haunt us."

The place was open for breakfast, but there were very few customers. Tommy and I saw Whitey's car pull up and park. He was the only one in the car. We entered the restaurant after Whitey. Jimmy Martorano led us out back to an inconspicuous table, away from other customers. Whitey looked calm and assured, as usual. Whitey sat with his back to the wall, looking the same as he had when we'd shaken hands that night outside the Transit, just before the war began. His skin-tight dungarees were held up with that shiny silver Alcatraz belt buckle. "Jimmy, were you guys shooting blanks the time you hit us on M Street?" I asked him with a slight grin. (We never called James Bulger "Whitey" to his face.)

I remember a forced pause. Tommy had his "I don't trust this asshole" face on; he stiffened as he looked at Whitey. I guess they weren't expecting me to break the ice with a reference to a botched assasination attempt.

"We couldn't believe we missed you. I think between the two of us we fired about thirty rounds into your car."

"Well you killed a lot of glass. I was picking it out of my hair the next morning in the shower."

I knew that Tommy's intuition that this would come back to haunt us was right on target. But we also had to end the shooting war. When a lot of people start getting murdered in broad daylight it tends to bring more police pressure. But as I looked over at Whitey sitting three feet from me, I couldn't imagine the extent of the mistake I was about to make in trusting him.

"No hard feelings. It's over," I reassured him. "But who was with you that day — Jimmy?" I still needed to make a mental note as to who actually pulled the trigger.

"Bobby was the other shooter and Jimmy drove." Whitey changed the subject quickly. "But what about the night over in Bunker Hill? That was a close one for both of us! If that little girl wasn't in my way . . . well . . ." He smirked.

He had a point, but I shot back: "I had you in my crosshairs, but with all the citizens around I couldn't take the chance. Thirty-ought-six rounds go a long, long way."

"When I saw you go to the bedroom I figured you had a rifle in there, and I sprinted. I remember thinking that I better keep moving. I knew you were a marine and you were in 'Nam. I thought, 'If he puts me into his crosshairs for one second, I'm down.'"

"I almost had you once, but I never got a clear shot. I couldn't afford a miss."

He laughed. "That's why I didn't take the shot while you were watching television. I had you dead but the little girl was in the room. I shouldn't have moved. Your eyes picked up the motion."

It was like talking about high school. There is real irony in meeting a deadly adversary after the fact. You get this surreal sense of connection, like the bond people form when they've shared a trauma.

Nobody talked fault, although at first it was tense while we ran down the "who killed who" list. Whitey was a defeated warrior looking to keep as much honor as possible. He knew the Mullens had courageous, fierce men willing to die for theirs, and he was perceptive. Deep down Whitey knew that he couldn't take over for the Killeens without cutting the Mullens in on their bookmaking and loan sharking. Tommy and I felt victorious, but we didn't want to gloat.

The meeting lasted for five or six hours. We ate good steaks, chasing them down with nothing stronger than ginger ale. It was business, and contrary to media stereotype, we weren't a bunch of lowlifes who sit around drinking beer all day and night. Things lightened up when I had to piss.

"Did you see *The Godfather*?" I asked Whitey.

"Yeah, four or five times," he responded.

"Well, do you remember when Michael gets up to piss during the meeting in the restaurant?"

He smiled and made a nervous attempt at a laugh. I stood up.

"We didn't have any guns when we came in, but would you like to check the bathroom? I gotta piss bad."

He just shook his head and smiled a little wider. I sensed that he wanted to trust me. But we were enemies — some things die hard. We had four guys with machine guns two blocks away and, we found out later, so did Whitey.

The balance of the meeting was spent forming an alliance, and by far the hardest part was deciding whom to protect. After a war each side usually gets to protect so many people from harm. Those who aren't protected are fair game for retribution and "shake-downs." Everything was split right down the middle. All the horses, dogs, bookmaking, and loan sharking were now going to be under our mutual control. This was the beginning of our relationship. Whitey and I were now officially partners and nobody at that table could have ever possibly imagined how this treacherous fuck would treat his partners. Nobody could have imagined that Whitey would spend many years in collusion with FBI agent John Connolly, ratting out many of his associates in return for being allowed to run his operation without interference from the feds. Connolly has been convicted, but Whitey is on the FBI's Most Wanted List, on the lam God knows where.

That double-cross was years away. The first test of our union came about a month later. I was eating at Mallows Tavern in South Station with Tommy King and a few other Mullens. One of the guys spotted Whitey pulling up alongside the bar. I went out alone. At first we just made small talk. It was nothing serious: Whitey and Jack Curran wanting to know how I was holding up under all this peace. We were like fighters feeling our way around the ring for the first few rounds. Neither one of us was completely sure of the other's intention.

"Pat, we need a third guy. You interested?" Whitey suddenly asked.

"What do you have?" I didn't see his request coming. I immediately tensed up.

"We got a problem up on Savin Hill," he replied. "We could use your help."

"Be right back. Just gotta tell the guys."

Jack was trying to read me but I wouldn't let him. I spun quickly and saw Tommy watching us through the window. Something wasn't right. I wondered if Whitey and Jack were trying to test my loyalty. They probably wanted to see how much of a partner I really was. Whitey figured if I would shoot somebody in Savin Hill for him, I was a true partner. I walked back inside without a trace of concern.

"They want me to go with them on a 'job.'" I wrapped my pinky and second finger against my palm, stuck my thumb out, and imitated a shot fired. Tommy understood.

"Don't go with them, Pat," he said. "It's not our problem."

"Tommy, we're either partners or we aren't. There is no better time than now to test this thing. I'm going. I'll be fine; don't worry."

I walked briskly, confidently, back outside to Whitey's car. I jumped in the backseat and we drove to a garage in Southie. Whitey had a boiler ready to go. Jack grabbed the bag of weapons while Whitey attached clean plates to the car. Whitey drove, I sat next to him, and Jack was directly behind me handing out the weapons. I wound up with a double-barreled shotgun, Whitey had a .45, and Jack had a 30.06 rifle. Each of us got a mask and gloves. Nobody said a word the entire ride to Dorchester.

After about an hour and half of sitting in a car up on Savin Hill I began to suspect a ruse. My skin began to crawl. It was now abundantly clear that there never was a problem. There never was a guy. I knew that no bookie would die this day. These guys were either here to kill me or they were testing me.

There's a certain smell to action, a certain adrenaline that's released into the air — and it wasn't there. Parked in Dorchester, Whitey started talking, mostly about himself. I pulled my baseball cap down over my eyes and slouched back in my seat. "Let me know when you need me guys; I'm getting some shut-eye," I said. I wanted to show them how relaxed I was, how sure in my belief that they didn't have the balls to kill me. But inside I was enraged. "Fuck you James J. Bulger! Did you forget my resolve? We won the shooting war, not you!"

Whitey finally realized I wasn't going for it and made up some excuse as we headed back to Southie. But he knew that I knew what his game was all about.

13. A CRIMINAL AND AN IRISHMAN

"I have always hated war and am by nature and philosophy
a pacifist, but it is the English who forced war upon us
and it is the first principle of war to kill the enemy."

— MAUD GONNE, Irish nationalist

In the 1970s South Boston was a great place to be
Irish. Everybody had family back in Ireland and, although most
came from the Republic in the south, we all became aware of the
abuses the Catholics in the North were being subjected to. So it
was only natural for much neighborly small talk to center around
the ongoing crisis in Northern Ireland. But you didn't see much of
the Troubles, as the crisis was being called, reported in the
American media — we heard about the persecution of Catholics in
the North from Irish newspapers or through word of mouth. To
this day many people in the States still have no clue about what the
British-backed Protestants have inflicted on my people. Job and
housing discrimination was the order of the day in the British-
controlled North. It was pure and simple bigotry — similar to
what American blacks went through in the fifties and sixties.

Let me digress for a quick history lesson. Back in the 1600s the
British government imported Scottish Presbyterians and English
Protestants to act as overlords to the native Irish. The Brits gave
the Protestants land and, more importantly, political power. The
Protestants ran the place for the Brits who, of course, were largely
Protestant as well. The Brits controlled the North by using the
imported Protestants as their proxies. When Michael Collins led

the IRA during the Anglo-Irish war of 1919–1921, forcing the British government — who at the time ruled all of Ireland — to relinquish their occupation of my country, the British held on to the six counties in the North. Why? Because that region was predominantly Protestant (because the Brits had made it so) *and* it was the most industrialized part of Ireland — that is, the most prosperous. Despite the fact that they've lived on the island of Ireland for generations, the Protestants consider themselves British, not Irish. And they're determined to keep things that way.

The Southie Irish all had one thing in common — we hated the English for what they had done and were still doing to the Irish. I'll never forget when I saw the videotapes of the Bloody Sunday massacre. It happened on January 30, 1972, in Derry. Twenty thousand people had been organized by the Northern Ireland Civil Rights Association to march peacefully to protest British policies of internment without trial. Mayhem erupted when British paratroopers rolled into the Bogside, a Catholic housing development, and just began wasting any Catholic in sight. Young or old, male or female, combatant or noncombatant, it didn't matter. If you were in the way, you died. Thirteen people were killed that day and fourteen were wounded, one of whom later died.

After that day the IRA's drive to destroy British control of Northern Ireland was, as you might imagine, powerful indeed.

My criminal activity and partnership with Whitey Bulger was growing stronger at this time, the same time that I was keeping a close eye on the situation in Northern Ireland. Not many days went by when I wasn't thinking of my people and their suffering. I had it easy — America was beautiful. We were all free. But I never forgot what my parents had endured trying to make ends meet back home, and that was without the oppression the Protestants were heaping on my Irish brothers in the North. I took nothing for granted.

In order to understand the current violations of human rights in Ireland, you have to first touch on a brief history of what the Irish people as a nation were forced to endure at the hands of the English. If you don't understand the history of England's oppression of Ireland, then all the IRA men and women who died fighting for Irish freedom are simply "terrorists," and that's just what people like Margaret Thatcher want you to believe. The English were butchers. In fact, if it wasn't for the IRA the British might well have wiped out the Irish people.

Let me begin at the beginning.

Henry II arrived in — well, let me call it what it was — Henry II and his army invaded Ireland in 1171, and by the end of the thirteenth century half of Ireland was under English rule. In 1366, concerned by the assimilation of Anglo-Norman settlers to Irish, or Gaelic, customs, the English issued a proclamation called the Statutes of Kilkenny. The statutes forbade speaking in Gaelic, dressing in an Irish manner, and adopting Irish names and law. The statutes forbade marriage between the Irish and Anglo-Norman settlers and banned Irish musicians and storytellers, and even went so far as to prohibit riding a saddle in anything other than the English manner and to ban the sport of hurling. The invaders did what all invaders do: they stripped us of our language and our culture, which means they tried to strip us of our identity. In fact, anybody caught speaking Gaelic risked imprisonment, the forfeiture of his land, or even execution.

James I of England established the Ulster Plantation in 1607, confiscating the six northern counties of Armagh, Cavan, Donegal, Fermanagh, Londonderry, and Tyrone for the Crown. Scottish Presbyterians and English Protestants were transported to Northern Ireland. In August of 1649, eight months after the execution of Charles I, the English Parliament sent Oliver Cromwell, then commander-in-chief and lord lieutenant, to Ireland to secure the rule of Parliament, and as implicit retribution for the Uprising of 1641, in which Catholics rose up against the Scots and English, killing some twelve thousand.

Cromwell landed in Dublin with an army over twenty thousand strong. At the siege of Drogheda, in September 1649, Cromwell massacred thirty-five hundred Irish men, women, and children and leveled the town; he followed this with the siege of Wexford, killing some fifteen hundred and razing that town. He issued an order that any Irish man, woman, or child caught east of the Shannon River would be executed. In March 1650, Cromwell and his troops surrounded the town of Kilkenny. Following negotiations, in which Cromwell demanded two thousand pounds in exchange for promising not to sack the town, Kilkenny surrendered.

By 1685, three-fourths of the land in Ireland and five-sixths of the houses belonged to the British. The continuation of Cromwell's policies — Cromwell had died in 1658 — reached genocidal proportions by midcentury. The policy of the English government in Ireland has consistently been that of divide and rule. From the 1690s through the end of the eighteenth century, the English imposed harsh penal laws throughout Ireland as well as in the United Kingdom, in an effort to suppress Catholic influence — "popery." Irish Catholics could not vote, could not become members of Parliament, could not send children abroad for education. They had no liberties — by law Irish Catholics could not own property, practice religion, or become literate by law.

In the late 1820s a major political effort for Irish freedom began to spread across the country. Daniel O'Connell, called The Liberator by many, led a nonviolent political movement in a valiant attempt to repeal all anti-Catholic legislation. The movement was referred to as the Catholic Liberation movement. He also lobbied for repeal of the Union Act of 1801, which forced Ireland into the United Kingdom. (Daniel O'Connell later became the first Catholic mayor of Dublin.) But the Great Famine put a decisive end to all hopes for Irish freedom.

The famine started in 1845 and ended in 1849, but the effects on the Irish people lasted for nearly two decades. The famine was so severe that it fractured the nation. Blight destroyed the potato crops, the staple food of over eight million tenant farmers. It is estimated that between seven hundred thousand and one million people died of starvation and disease. Another one million escaped death by coming to America, while a million more emigrated in following decades. No United Nations came to the aid of the Irish; in fact, English absentee landlords continued to export Irish grain to England for profit. They evicted families that could no longer pay rent and tore down their houses so they couldn't be reoccupied.

But resolve and resilience are two qualities innate to the Irish. In 1867 we dusted ourselves off and got back to business. A small band of revolutionaries known as the Fenians rose up against British rule, in the hope that recognition of their plight — and aid — would come from the United States. The English government sent aid and weapons to the Confederate Army during the American Civil War; surely the United States would understand the Irish fight for freedom and return the favor. But Washington failed to give the Fenians a second look.

It was a small group of Irish who had managed to escape the famine that put together the first recorded shipment of arms to Irish freedom fighters. *Erin's Hope*, a wooden vessel loaded with weapons and thirty-eight volunteers, set sail in April 1867 from New York. But by the time the ship hit shore in Sligo, the uprising had been soundly defeated and the leaders marched off to prison.

On Easter Sunday, 1916, the poorly armed IRA led an attack on several strategic points in Dublin. They captured the General Post Office and hours later the green, white, and orange Irish flag flew from the roof. However, after a week of fighting the IRA had to surrender. They had taken on the Brits in a conventional war — which was a big mistake, since the Brits had gunboats, artillery, and superior numbers. But they wouldn't make that mistake again — Michael Collins would later see to that.

James Connolly and Padraig Pearse, two prominent leaders of

the rebellion, were executed. In fact, Connolly was so severely wounded during the Easter Week fighting that he could not stand. He was executed by a British firing squad while sitting in a chair. History shows that this was the biggest mistake the English ever made. It awakened the Irish nation. The cry for freedom was heard around Ireland. IRA members were about to become Ireland's favorite sons and daughters.

Republican resistance intensified in the countryside, where the now-unified Irish Republican Army and its new leader, Michael Collins, began the quest for freedom. Collins brought urban guerilla warfare to Ireland. He saw clearly that engaging the Brits in a straight-up conventional battle was suicide, and used intelligence gathering on the British security forces to terrorize them. His strategy eventually wore down the enemy and they sought a way out of Ireland. The resulting treaty, which was hotly debated by various Irish political leaders, created the Republic of Ireland — but it also created the British controlled Northern Ireland.

Ever since then, Irish Republicans — people like the Catholics in the North, the IRA, my parents, and me — have longed to reunite our country. Ireland — with its own Gaelic language and customs intact and without the dispossession of its people's land and other British atrocities — would be much better off.

My parents were both Republicans: they hated the British for what they had done. My father was a dedicated Free Stater. One memory I'll never forget is the sound of a late-night family get-together in Southie, with my father playing the accordion as my mother led everybody in the crowded room in a chorus of the famous Irish fight song "The Risin' of the Moon."

Southie had a huge Northern Aid organization. A man named John Connelly (no relation to the FBI agent who helped Whitey Bulger bring down all his "friends") headed a group of IRA sympathizers out of his storefront on Broadway. Connelly was a burly, vibrant, honorable Irishman who spoke of nothing else but getting back for Ireland what was rightfully hers to begin with.

Nobody ever questioned Connelly's commitment. In fact, in Southie he became the conscience of Northern Ireland's struggle for freedom. John collected donations; he never got deeply involved in or paid attention to what the money was used for. His son-in-law, Peter Curran, was the go-to guy for organizing more radical means of support.

Since 1969 I'd been following the civil rights movement that started in Northern Ireland, but only with one eye. My main goal back then was to get the man who took my brother Peter from us. So although I had a longstanding interest in Ireland, my first loyalty was to my parents and carrying out what they wanted me to do — avenge my brother's death.

That same year, 1969, was the year the Irish decided to put an end to discrimination in Northern Ireland. The Catholics had been systematically excluded from participating in virtually all but the lowest occupations in both the public and private sectors. Housing was allocated by a patronage system; without exception the Catholics were given substandard living arrangements. England had passed the Special Powers Act after the 1916 Uprising; any unrest whatsoever led to arrest and prison without trial or legal charges for anyone suspected of being an IRA member or supporter. In many cases people were imprisoned for simply talking about unfair treatment and freedom.

The present conflict in Ireland is often framed as a religious conflict or as a holy war. If you ask a random one hundred Americans, the overwhelming majority will tell you it's a religious battle that will never end. In fact, I've had several people liken the situation in Northern Ireland to that in Israel or to the war in Bosnia, but nothing could be farther from the truth.

Unfortunately, these gross misconceptions have prevented a lot of Americans from taking a closer look at the struggle. In Northern Ireland the terms "Catholic" and "Protestant" are merely labels. It just works out that most Catholics happen to be Nationalist — they believe in a united Ireland, without any British presence. The Protestants, or Unionists, are descendants of the Scotsmen and English that the British planted in Ireland to run things; naturally the Protestants are loyal to their British benefactors, and so they believe in a continued union with England.

The IRA and the Irish Nationalists, or Republicans, are fighting for a cause: they want to unite Ireland with the British-controlled North. Ireland is an island; it is a singular entity with a homogeneous population. Yet six counties in the north of Ireland are part of Great Britain, not Ireland!

My first real action in the Republican struggle was to raise money for NORAID. I'd go to John Connelly and ask him about NORAID's financial needs. He might tell me they needed a couple grand to help some IRA soldier who needed a safe place to hide. It never took me long to provide Connelly what he wanted. The bookies knew — if you wanted to operate in Southie it was in your best interest to support the Irish cause.

In early 1974, after a few years of supporting the Irish struggle in this way, I went to Whitey and told him I wanted to get more deeply involved. I wanted to alert him of my priority shift and I wanted a commitment of time and money from our operations. At first Whitey couldn't warm to the idea of something that didn't involve Southie and didn't put money in his pocket. But as I peppered Whitey with factual accounts that Connelly would pass on to me on a daily basis, he began to reconsider.

Outraged at the torture of my people at the hands of British soldiers, I became active in the South Boston community by operating under the radar. As a criminal, and quietly, you could do a lot to help the IRA. But I didn't have to sell the idea that hard — the British took care of that for me. Their inhumane treatment of suspected IRA activists and the brutality of their policies in Northern Ireland were most effective recruiting tools. Money poured into NORAID like water from a faucet every time Connelly brought more facts to our attention.

Between July 1972 and December 1973, the British army recovered 1,329 weapons of various kinds, including 665 rifles, 62 machine guns, 449 handguns, 169 shotguns, 10 rocket launchers, and 14 mortars in Ireland and Europe from suspected IRA soldiers. During that same time period they seized over 150,000 rounds of ammunition. Things were quite dark. The freedom fighters were now losing more guns than they were receiving. Word got back to Southie that the IRA was suffering its worst setback in many years.

The English government became desperate to find more than guns. The British army was ordered to carry out a massive search for suspected IRA members. The Brits rounded up one thousand Catholic men and held them in jails, on a prison ship, and in two rural concentration camps. Word soon got back to Connelly that the prisoners were being tortured. That got Whitey's attention. For all of his swagger and bravado, Whitey's fascination with torture told the truth about who he was inside. It's cowards who get a sick thrill out of inflicting pain on helpless people.

But the Brits had the wrong guys. The IRA had been tipped off before the British began their search; most of the IRA leaders had already gone into hiding, scattered across the twenty-six counties of the Republic. Most of the men interned were guilty of nothing more than leading civil rights protests. In fact, those leaders had studied and followed many of the nonviolent tactics of the American civil rights movement of the 1960s.

I'll never forget the time Connelly introduced Whitey and me to a man from Northern Ireland who had managed to escape the British clampdown and flee to Boston. He was a well-known Irish amateur fighter. I became sick listening to his stories; I was so filled with rage my stomach ached.

The British army grabbed him coming out of a pub one night in early January 1971. He'd been sitting alone in a room for hours when three men with stockings over their faces burst in. The head guy said to him, "If you want things to go easy from here, you'd best tell us everything you've done." But of course there was nothing to tell. They knew he was Catholic and that was guilt enough for them. He told Whitey and me how they'd stood him against a wall with fingers and legs outstretched. They proceeded to kick him in the stomach and groin for nearly thirty minutes. Each time he went down they picked him up and ordered him against the wall.

I remember the story because I wanted one minute alone with the three of them at once — the fucking cowards. I guess one time after they knocked him down they pulled off his pants. He said they were having a good old time laughing at him naked on the floor. Then one stood on his throat, one held his legs apart, and the other lit several matches. He blew the matches out and touched them to the guy's penis. One of them made a few remarks about his wife and forced him to his feet.

The poor bastard — it wasn't over.

I glanced over at Whitey as the IRA guy was telling his story and could see him becoming sucked in. But I didn't trust him, nor did I know at the time of his propensity for torture. Later I'd come to understand that he got off on it.

The boxer then told us that they had brought him to another room, blindfolded him, and injected him with some sort of drug. He felt something like a blood pressure cuff around his arm and then was immediately hit with a jolt of electricity. The next thing he remembered was waking up naked on the floor of a cell that he was to call home for the next nine months. Needless to say, that man became an IRA activist once he got out of prison.

Connelly also told me about what happened to Edward Duffy, Gerald Donnelly, and Gerard Bradley in Armagh Prison. They were Belfast men who'd been arrested in 1972 and refused to confess to something they had no part in. They were so brutally beaten that a prison doctor had to cut their trousers off to diagnose and treat their injuries. Two of them had fractured arms, and all three had to be admitted to the local hospital.

Over the next several years I became more deeply planted in South Boston's Irish mob. In addition, Stevie Flemmi (more on him in a minute) had an operation in Roxbury and I had my feet in Charlestown. Back one night in the early 1970s, an Irishman named Joe Cahill showed up at a bar now known as Triple O's Lounge on Broadway. Joe was a legendary IRA commander — a founder in 1969 of the Provisional IRA — to whom the American government had refused to extend a visa. The Brits really wanted to get their hands on Joe Cahill. However, the IRA had friends in Canada, and lazy border patrols made for an easy entrance.

Peter Curran was plugged in; even Whitey was amazed when he was introduced to Cahill. Joe had a deep, ruddy, wind-cut look from spending much of his life in the cold Irish countryside. The deep wrinkles gave more away than just age. He was a legend who spoke of peace in Ireland, not about how many British soldiers he had killed (which was all Whitey wanted to know about). But Joe warned of a period of bloodshed before unification and peace could be achieved. He asked for our assistance in bringing that peace to a quick reality — which meant supplying him with weapons. Now. Joe was a gentleman warrior, someone we greatly respected and were willing to help. Plus, we were criminals, which meant we had access to all kinds of weapons.

I felt that helping the Irish was the right thing to do. After all, I was reaping the benefits of American patriots who'd kicked the shit out of the Brits for trying to do the same thing here in America as the Brits were now doing (and had been doing for centuries) to the Irish.

When I told Whitey of my passionate commitment and my desire to support the IRA, he appeared moved, but somehow his response seemed shallow and insincere. I think he liked the legitimacy a political cause gave him; I sure know he didn't give a hoot about my people. He gave me his blessing, but it was all just lip service. And it didn't matter anyhow; he knew my determination once I'd committed to something — what could he do to stop me? It was in his best interest to support my cause.

Whitey and I were still in complete control of South Boston, but by now he had introduced Stevie "The Rifleman" Flemmi into the equation. Stevie was of average height with black hair, brown eyes, and a pasty olive complexion. Gerry Angiulo had given Whitey the nod on Stevie. I'd heard he'd been involved in the 1968 Fitzgerald car bombing, in which a Boston attorney representing a mob hitman had lost his leg. Flemmi had skipped out on an indictment and gone on the lam in Canada, where he'd stayed until 1974. Stevie's friend Frankie Salemme had taken the hit for it and was doing time at Cedar Junction in South Walpole, Massachusetts. One day it just seemed to happen — Stevie became attached to Whitey's hip.

Nobody knew then that they were both working for the FBI. Years later we heard that Stevie became an informant the day he stepped off the boat from his military service in Korea. It was a funny thing — I could never really warm up to him. To the best of my recollection I don't believe I had more than a dozen conversations with him from the mid-1970s to when Whitey went on the lam in 1996 and Stevie, for reasons known only to him, stayed behind and was arrested.

Gerry Angiulo was a smart guy, but Whitey and Stevie were protected by the FBI. In fact, Stevie hadn't been a fugitive in Canada

— truth be told, he'd been hidden there by the feds. They'd then brought him back to Boston to team with Whitey because he was the best rat they had ever had.

In 1975 the course of my life was changed forever by two events. First, I married Debbie Gunn, a beautiful blonde Southie girl with blue eyes. We had been dating for over a year and decided to make it official so that we could start a family. The second incident was the turning point in my work for the IRA.

It was a warm night around eleven o'clock. I'd just come back from a meeting with Whitey in which we'd discussed our forceful correction of two bookies who were skimming off the top. I turned on the late news and saw helicopters evacuating the American embassy in Saigon. Men and women with babies were climbing over each other trying to grab a young Marine's outstretched hand.

In the background you could hear the rat-tat-tat of automatic weapons, AK-47s, a sound I knew well. Panic was everywhere. We'd lost the war.

I almost cried remembering the young Southie guys who had died fighting to secure freedom and justice for the Vietnamese. Now we were retreating in shame. Too many of my brother marines had died for absolutely nothing.

I can still feel the electricity that shot through my legs. I felt as if I'd woken up from a sound sleep ready for action. The entire room seemed to fill with light. I realized right then and there that I could make a difference in Northern Ireland. I knew if I worked hard, and at any cost, I'd be able to help my people. I just couldn't sit around and watch what happened in Vietnam happen in Northern Ireland.

It was old John Connelly who faithfully encouraged me. I think he must have spotted me, picked me out of the crowd, because he'd heard about my implacable desire for revenge against those who crossed me or my family. He knew my mother and father and had seen how determined I was to avenge Peter's murder.

Connelly understood the rules of engagement for people who played at my level. He understood that some guys talk and some guys listen — the dangerous guys are the ones who listen, the ones who don't talk but who act. John Connelly taught me that Northern Ireland was a war we could win; the United States Marine Corps taught me how I could make that possible.

Machine guns, mortars, bullets, and intelligence are what win wars. There was no question — I knew that I had to step up to the plate. I had to go to the next level and bring the IRA the weapons it needed to win.

14. THE LONG JOURNEY HOME

My wife, Debbie, and I moved into a one-bedroom apartment on the corner of N and Eighth. In 1975 our daughter Shannon was born and we moved over to P and Broadway, to an apartment with another bedroom. Our second daughter, Shauna, was born in 1980, about the same time that things went big.

By now word of my commitment to Irish freedom was beginning to spread throughout IRA circle — I'd receive a request for cash and I'd fill it. Peter Curran began taking me to locations throughout Boston and New York to meet IRA volunteers hiding in America. I liken the loyalty and commitment of these volunteers to that of a father looking out for his only son. They were, in a word, impressive. Committed, well-trained, and resourceful, these IRA men were guys I liked being around.

One thing became dramatically clear. The IRA men I was helping were nothing like Whitey Bulger and Stevie Flemmi. These men killed because they were in a war; England had taken their country and they were going to get it back. Unlike Whitey, they didn't talk about themselves and how many young girls they'd had. In fact, they didn't talk much at all.

Peter Curran rubbed Whitey the wrong way. Stevie and Whitey thought he was a bit pretentious. That was rich! You see, Whitey was the most egocentric criminal I'd ever met. He made sure you knew that he'd done this or been a part of that. He loved to hear himself talk about himself! Peter Curran was a committed, decent Irishman. Yes, Peter was on the verge of being a fanatic. A few times I had to let him know he was preaching to the choir. But he believed in something bigger than himself, something Whitey and Stevie would never understand. Life for those two was all about money, image, and women — young women, usually.

The biggest difference between Whitey and the IRA was the IRA volunteers' willingness to die. They would never call for a truce or a deal. They had honor and courage.

IRA volunteers frequently said "peace by violence"; they used violence as a political tool. On the other hand, for Whitey and Stevie violence was not a tool; it was recreation. They loved to inflict pain on others even when a stern talking to would have gotten the desired result. Mostly, though, they only did things that in some way put money in their pockets or enhanced their mystique in South Boston.

In 1981 the situation in Ireland got serious. In the course of the five years previous the British government had taken 250 suspected IRA men into custody. Most were incarcerated in the infamous Long Kesh Prison outside Belfast, also known as "the Maze." (Long Kesh was shut down in 2000.) All alleged IRA men were locked up in the infamous H-blocks where, having been denied Special Category status as political prisoners by the British government, they wore nothing but bedsheets or blankets. They simply refused to wear the uniforms provided for criminals, since each and every man being held demanded to be categorized as a political prisoner.

On March 1, 1981, Bobby Sands began his hunger strike. Sands was a political genius. He saw that the world at large was prejudiced against the IRA and its methods because of the British control of the media. Sands saw that the IRA would always be portrayed as bloodthirsty killers until IRA volunteers could show the world otherwise.

Bloodthirsty killers hold nothing higher in their minds than their own self-interest. Bobby Sands showed the world that he and his fellow IRA volunteers held a higher ideal. What men those hunger strikers were! They showed Margaret Thatcher and the people of England and Ireland that they weren't thugs and murderers, that they were warriors fighting for a noble and just cause.

Thatcher, who was the British prime minister from 1979 to 1990, was despised by the Irish Republicans beyond anything you can imagine. Incarcerated IRA members wanted status as political prisoners; Thatcher called them common — though brutal — criminals. She treated men who were fighting a war against the British occupation of Northern Ireland as thieves, drug dealers, and murderers. She actually said "There is no such thing as political murder, political bombing, or political violence. There is only criminal murder, criminal bombing, and criminal violence. We will not compromise on this. There will be no political status." Really? British history is full of incidents in which the English killed to achieve their political ends. Of course, the Brits are no different than any other country in this, but the hypocrisy in calling the IRA volunteers murderers, with all that blood — a lot of it Irish — on the British Empire's hands is sickening. Thatcher allowed ten IRA volunteers to die because of the color of their prison uniforms, because they wore bedsheets.

Bobby Sands inspired us all. How could anyone — outside of the British government, naturally — not be impressed by this man's commitment? Sands was nominated for a seat in the Irish Parliament and was easily elected on April 9, 1981 — on day 40 of his hunger strike. Most importantly, Bobby Sands' actions brought about a huge shift in public opinion worldwide regarding the IRA and its cause. What were these ten men willing to starve themselves to death for? They all died for something beyond themselves.

Every week John Connelly and other supporters would distribute transcripts of the words Sands wrote from his prison cell. Sands' courage was multiplying the ranks of IRA volunteers. Most of us were humbled by Bobby Sands' commitment, and we were forced to find something inside ourselves that could match even a fraction of his courage.

I remember hearing accounts of Bobby Sands' last hours. Jim Gibney, a prominent figure in Sinn Fein, the IRA's political wing, had just visited him. Sands was weak. He was in the company of his mother and his sister.

"How are you?" asked Gibney.

"Is that you, Jim?" Sands responded.

"It is, Bobby." Gibney took Bobby's hand.

"I'm blind. I can't see you. Tell the lads to keep their chins up."

Later that day it was reported that Bobby Sands' left eye was black and closed, the right eye was nearly closed, and his mouth was twisted, as though he had had a stroke. He had no feeling in his legs and could only speak in whispers. The pain is his stomach caused unceasing dry retching. Finally, Bobby Sands uttered his last words: "Well, that's it. Keep my ma in mind."

After sixty-six days on hunger strike, Bobby Sands died on May 5, 1981. Some one hundred thousand people attended his funeral in Belfast. Nine more hunger strikers had died by the end of August 1981. The six surviving hunger strikers ended their strike in October, and a week later the British government ceded to one of their key requests: to be allowed to wear their own clothes.

Had Thatcher had a change of heart? Or did she simply realize she'd been exposed as negligently willful when it came to the IRA?

While it was over for Bobby Sands, it was just the start for me and countless others who grew stronger and stronger as nine more men followed Sands to the grave inside Long Kesh.

Between 1974 and 1978 we had had tremendous success smuggling arms in coffins. South Boston and Charlestown were filled with people who had left Ireland in search of a better life. But everybody gets old and everybody dies. You'd be surprised how many of those folks wanted to be buried on their own sod. I had a friend from Charlestown who was an undertaker, and not one family member ever knew what else traveled over the ocean with their loved ones' bodies.

Caskets were ideal for smuggling rifles. You didn't need much space. We were able to get at least five rifles, a couple of handguns, and some ammunition under a corpse. But the obvious downside was that we had to wait for somebody who wanted to be buried back in Ireland to die.

I made an all-out commitment to support the IRA's cause at whatever cost. I began to feel frustrated because I knew my expertise and training as a Marine, combined with my position with the Irish mob, could provide the IRA with better resources. I refused to let this become another Vietnam. I put the word out to John that I was ready for the next level. A month later Peter Curran showed up on my doorstep. He informed me that the IRA wanted me to visit Ireland. This was just what I was fishing for, and from that point on I never looked back.

Two weeks later I was flown to Ireland to meet with what I took to be some upper-mid-level IRA leaders.

By this time Debbie and I had split up. I brought my girlfriend at the time, Mary Nee, along for the trip. Back then she traveled everywhere with me. She was a tiger, a beautiful girl — a brunette with a firm body and mischief in her eyes. It was perfect — she was no relation to me but she had the same last name. Customs agents thought we were married; a husband and wife on vacation never drew any suspicions.

It was quite strange looking out the window of our plane as we approached Dublin. I was finally home. I had been back once before, in 1978, with my mother and father, but this time it was business. I had visions of Ma stoking the fire to keep us warm, Dad sitting on the pub stool in Galway. It was funny how things turned out for my family. We left Ireland because we were poor. America gave us a chance. I became a United States Marine and fought in Vietnam, and then I became a successful thief, one who later was positioned by a gang war into being a gangster. Now I was about to meet the IRA in my homeland. My mother and father were Republicans to the very core; in a way, I was doing this for them. They really were proud of my activities.

I'd been given instructions to stay at the Shelbourne Hotel in Dublin. I was told only to wait until somebody came for me in the bar. I sat alone at the same table every day and drank nothing but tea. For three days Mary and the bartender talked bullshit, but one afternoon in the bar I was alone; Mary was still sleeping, probably hungover. I noticed a new young waiter. At first he wouldn't make eye contact. Then he came to my table and quickly handed me a handwritten note with elaborate instructions.

The meeting was set for that night in the outskirts of Dundalk, an hour's drive north from Dublin on the coast. The instructions asked me to leave the hotel at 8 P.M., get in my rented car, wait for a black Ford to pull out in front of me, and follow its lead. I was told to turn off my lights when the black Ford turned off its lights, to turn off my engine and glide when the Ford turned off its engine and glided. That was it — it seemed somewhat ominous but simple. I returned to my room and relaxed. I felt good. I was on my way to doing something for the cause.

I left Mary around 7:45. She'd already been in the downstairs tavern trying to heal her wounds from the night before. I really liked Mary. She never asked questions, so she knew nothing of my business.

It was a fresh fall evening; the cool Irish air felt great against my face. The blackness of the night was a powerful reminder of why I was such a good criminal — I was never scared of the unknown. In fact, it excited me. I jumped into my rented car, started it up, and waited. It seemed like just a matter of seconds before the black

Ford Escort pulled out of an alleyway and hopped in front of me. I hit my lights and we headed out of Dublin.

I think we must have driven for ninety minutes or so before we turned toward the coast. Clearly we weren't taking a direct route. There were two figures inside the black Ford. My headlights illuminated their shoulders and the backs of their heads with a dull yellow glow; I couldn't tell if they were young or old. As we drove the air got colder; we were getting deeper into the country. I'd never experienced such darkness. The fields stretched for miles on either side. Every ten minutes I'd see a distant light that made the outline of the farmhouses a different shade of black.

Finally the Ford slowed and cut its lights. I did the same. The driver turned right and cut his engine. I put my car into neutral, cut the engine, and coasted with them down a steep roadway. I could see the silhouette of a farmhouse looming larger in front of me. We coasted into the yard.

I waited. The two men opened their doors and I followed. Nobody spoke. Two figures with rifles, facing away from me, stood by the front door. I couldn't tell what caliber the rifles were — the darkness made it difficult to see. Once inside the farmhouse the two guys from the car kept going right out the back door. I never saw their faces.

"Pat."

Somebody knew me.

I felt a tingle of anticipation down my spine. When I turned I saw an old friend I'd helped hide in Southie. He looked refreshed; his face wasn't so tense and drained. But those eyes: those midnight eyes still spoke volumes.

I followed him to a sitting room off the kitchen. Bread, butter, tea, milk, and sugar were laid out on the table next to the couch. The fireplace was roaring with a turf fire that filled the room with a strong, fresh fragrance. I loved that smell. It was one of the strongest memories I'd kept from my childhood in Ireland.

There were six men around the fire that night. The room was lit only by the firelight bouncing off the walls. It was all very cozy, really, although a sense of urgency was palpable. On my left were two country farmers in their midfifties. They each wore woolen sport coats, vests, and white shirts. But what I remember the most were their hard, calloused hands. On my right were two younger men in sweaters. They didn't say much, but they were extremely intense. My friend who'd stayed with me in South Boston made most of the small talk. He was close to forty, well educated, dressed casually in loafers and slacks. I'll never forget how he lit one cigarette off the other the entire night.

The meeting lasted until dawn. We talked detail after detail about guns — operations were never disclosed, of course, but specific instances, such as an ambush, would be named when discussing the best guns for a given situation. And of course we addressed how the guns would be smuggled into Europe — France was the desired port of entry — and how they would be retrieved from there. Every possible angle was covered. I wasn't used to weighing every step like this, at least not in this wide scope. In Southie we just made things happen — it was our turf. Ireland was home for these men, but given the British army's presence, it was hostile territory. Southie was ours; even some of the cops gave us a break. But this was different.

We talked about what I could do for these men. They were well aware of my Irish birth, so they felt comfortable simply telling me what they needed. I found that flattering; they trusted me. It made me feel as though I belonged. They had three major issues. The younger guys spoke of the specific weapons they needed. They went to great lengths to emphasize how quickly they needed AK-47s, C-4 plastic explosives, and electronic detonators. The old, rugged farmers talked for hours about a possible delivery system — how to get the guns into the younger guys' hands. They had had great luck in the past with oversized furniture containers their volunteers had picked up off freighters from French ports. The third issue was money. My friend wanted me to take care of the finances. These guys were freedom fighters. Money had no meaning but for the purpose of buying weapons.

The meeting ended just as morning light began creeping in through the windowpanes. I heard tea boiling in the kitchen. One of the old farmers stood up and, with that, one at a time, we all followed. I nodded to my friend, shook all their hands, and moved toward the door I'd come through the night before. The morning rays lit up the dust particles. The place looked different in the light of day. The kitchen seemed bigger and much colder. The woolen sweaters hanging on hooks by the back door reminded me of my childhood, the way my mother carefully hung up my father's coats. Although Dundalk was on the east coast, on the other side of Ireland from Galway, being here brought back memories.

I couldn't stop thinking about how the hell I was going to deliver the goods. These guys needed me. They trusted me. I had to figure it out — and I would. I remember driving up the steep hill to the main road. The brilliant green moss fields were covered with foggy dew. The sun coming over the hills was beautiful. This was Ireland.

Back in Southie it took me only a few weeks to gather up my Irish friends' entire weapons list. They wanted thirty automatic rifles, twenty-five handguns, ten blocks of C-4 explosives, and twenty-five hundred in rounds of ammunition, and even that wouldn't put a dent in their total needs. I broke up the order into sections and stored them in the basements of IRA sympathizers around Boston. Now I had to find a van and somebody with the expertise to modify it to hide weapons so the packed van could make it to Ireland.

It didn't even take a month. I found my man at a rally for Northern Aid in Charlestown. Actually, Whitey and I had used him before. He was a young and determined auto body repair specialist who had installed release buttons on a few of the backseats of the hot cars we'd use for jobs around Southie. He'd hollow out a spot behind the backseat and mount a release button out of easy reach. You couldn't accidentally hit this button, believe me. And there was no way to get the backseat down without pushing this button. We kept our weapons — or large sums of money — there as we drove to and from whatever mayhem we had created.

It had never dawned on me to ask this guy for help, but seeing him suddenly gave me the idea. I walked right up to him in the middle of the street, as nonchalant as though I were bumming a cigarette. I asked if he'd be interested in helping me after the meeting. He told me to stop by the shop and fill him in.

The next day I pulled out my list and showed him the cargo. This kid was pure genius. "Buy a new Dodge van," he replied. "I'll show you what I can do."

Within a week the van was sitting in his shop. It just happened that Dodge made their vans with several inches of dead floor space. I still have no clue as to why they did that, but we loved it.

First we weighed and measured the van with no additional weight inside — just as it had rolled out of the factory. We took Polaroids of the back and front, above and underneath. Then we established the weight of the weapons and changed the shocks to compensate. Then this kid went to work cutting and realigning the interior. He measured the height of the seats and cut four inches off the legs. He raised the floor by suspending hydraulics with piano hinges. He purchased carpet that was identical to the factory issue and cemented it carefully to the raised floor. After comparing the before pictures to the after shots and making sure everything matched up, he remounted the seats.

I rounded up the weapons and we packed everything neatly in greased bags so nothing would rust. It took us all night to arrange and rearrange the weapons so that they fit inside the new floor space. Then we insulated everything with warm foam that would harden into a kind of casing, preventing the weapons from shifting in transit. Now all he had to do was bolt huge screws through the new floor to keep everything perfectly tight. By morning the van was ready to travel.

I'd already filled out all the necessary papers to ship the van from Newark, New Jersey, to the English Channel port of Le Havre. We'd found a shipping schedule for a Polish freighter. It was perfect and cheap. There was nothing left to do but get the van to its port of departure. I wanted my hands on this first effort; I wanted to make sure it went off as we planned. I shook my auto body genius friend's hand firmly and headed down the highway. I'll never forget the five-hour ride to the loading dock, thinking of nothing but those fifty pounds of C-4s and fifteen electric detonators right underneath the seat.

I pulled up to the United States customs station and three agents stepped out to meet me. I wasn't nervous; it was like going through a tollbooth. These guys were just doing their job, and they certainly weren't looking for guns loaded in a van going to the IRA. The Dodge van had plenty of windows; they could see inside easily, and there was nothing to hide. There was no reason for anybody to be suspicious or ask me to open anything. All they wanted to do was to make sure the paperwork was up to date, with all the necessary signatures to cover their asses. One of them jumped inside and drove the van down to the freighter that would take it to France.

I went back to Boston and waited a day or two before flying to Paris. I had to give the IRA the information on the van and the freighter's arrival as soon as possible. I could have stayed home, but I'd committed myself to guaranteeing delivery.

I waited for the IRA contact at a little café in a train station in Paris. I went alone this time. It wasn't the time to play tourist with Mary. The place was wall-to-wall people; again it took about a day and a half for the spotter to feel safe enough to approach me. Finally an IRA guy I'd met in Ireland sat down next to me. I spent a few days with him until the ship came in. We didn't talk much. Each day was the same: we'd eat, drink tea, and walk the streets. But then it was time to leave Paris. It took us a little under four hours to reach Le Havre.

When we finally arrived my friend said something in French to the inspector, who laughed and whistled the gate open. As we drove away I remember a feeling of victory: I was finally doing something tangible to help the Irish take back Ireland. I'd done other things for my people, but this was significant.

But it wasn't the most important thing I'd do. There was something bigger coming.

15. THE BIRTH OF *VALHALLA*

Whitey started to become paranoid after the van deal. He asked me to shut down all operations for the IRA. He didn't like me spending so much of my time in Charlestown with guys sympathetic to the Irish struggle. I think Whitey feared that I might develop new — read that as *dangerous* — alliances. Dangerous to Whitey, that is. Whitey never hung much in Charlestown — he found my Charlestown connections too wild, too unpredictable. I think he sensed that those Townies didn't like him, and he was right. You have to give it to Whitey, he has good instincts. That's why he's still on the run.

In fact, it was the Charlestown guys who first told me Whitey was a homosexual. One weekend I informed Whitey that I was going to the Cape. Billy Sheehan, a Charlestown guy and one of the best men I ever knew — they simply don't come any more solid than Billy — and four or five other Townies had rented a cottage in Hyannis. Whenever Whitey didn't like something he looked downward. I remember him looking down when I told him I was going to the Cape, and then looking over at Stevie Flemmi. "Sure, sure," he said. But his qualified approval meant he was worried about me spending time with the Charlestown guys.

Down in Hyannis, late in the afternoon, the boys and I were playing cards and drinking in the living room. One of the Townies spotted a car with two guys sitting in it about fifty feet from the house. Billy took out his binoculars and seconds later began laughing hysterically. One by one they all took turns looking at the two men who were watching our house: it was Whitey and Kevin Weeks.

Kevin was a great kid; he was young and loyal. Whitey, twenty-eight years his senior, had recruited him right out of high school.

Kevin had no criminal background; he was just a kid who'd gotten sucked in by Bulger's ego and loved being the guy next to Whitey. Who could blame him? Whitey was a legend in Southie, make no mistake about that. There were dozens of kids who would have killed — yes, quite literally — to be where Kevin was. I liked Kevin a lot. We'd studied Uechi-ryu karate together until Whitey decided Kevin was spending too much time away from him. Too bad. Kevin was talented.

Billy looked at me with a mischievous glint in his eye. "Let's have some fun," he said. "Pat, go down there and invite 'em in for a few drinks."

"Are you sure you want Whitey in here?" I asked.

"Definitely. Let's mess with 'em," somebody replied.

I walked down slowly, trying to keep a straight face. I was tempted to sneak up on them from behind, but then I realized that there was a very real possibility that surprising Whitey might get me shot. So I scratched that idea. Whitey saw me, and I knew he and Kevin were going over strategy, their reason for being there. Whitey had such an ego, but he had absolutely no skill as a stalker whatsoever; he wasn't in plain sight, but his attempt at surveillance was clumsy. He hadn't brought binoculars that would have enabled him to be far enough away to avoid being spotted. What was he thinking? Here we are, pure criminals on a beachfront in Hyannis. Didn't he imagine we'd look out the window for feds? Or even for the local police? When you've been a criminal for a while, that's hardwired into you: you check your surroundings constantly.

"Jimmy? That you?"

"Hey Pat. Just making sure you're alright."

"Brilliant," I thought, "like I'd have trouble with the Charlestown guys." Still, it was a decent excuse given the tension between him and the Townies. Whitey smiled nervously.

"Come on in. Drive up and park in the driveway."

"No, we just dropped by to make sure everything was okay," he said, sounding more convincing the second time.

"It's only Billy, Tommy, and a few other guys. They're great guys. Come on, have some laughs," I said, chuckling.

I opened the back door of Whitey's midnight-blue Ford LTD, slid into the backseat, and tapped Kevin a hello on the shoulder. Whitey reluctantly drove up to the house. Whitey and Kevin followed me in. The boys already had their plan in motion. Billy had dumped a bag of cocaine out onto the glass coffeetable. Joey was rolling a joint and had a cellophane bag filled with blonde buds resting on his lap. Somebody else had planted two bottles of Scotch right in the middle of the table. I tried not to smile; it would ruin everything.

"Jimmy!" they all greeted Whitey at once.

Billy leaned over the table with a rolled up twenty dollar bill in his nose and hit a huge line of coke. The swishing sound cut the tension in the room. Whitey joined the circle but wouldn't take a drink. Joey sparked the end of the joint, and sweet, white smoke swirled around the overhead fan. It must have been a couple of hours before Whitey finally accepted a drink. The guys just talked nonsense, being as crude as possible. You see, Whitey loved being viewed as an intellectual who read Clausewitz and saw foreign movies. A smart guy? Oh, yes. A genius? No. The feds were the ones who made Whitey untouchable, not Whitey himself. And the Townies knew he wasn't Albert Einstein, so they cranked up the trash talk. Frankie made up a few stories about hot-looking girls in the Bunker Hill Projects and Billy kept asking Whitey to tell him stories about Alcatraz.

Whitey decided to leave around eight in the evening and shook everybody's hand. As soon as we heard their car pull away, we lit the place up with laughter.

"I wonder if he's really queer," Billy stated.

"Does Jimmy Bulger go that way?" Joey coughed out a response as he passed the joint to Frankie.

"I never saw it," I replied. "And I've been around him. He likes really young broads." That was accurate — I knew that for a fact.

"Do you know Hank Garrity, the bookie?" Billy stood and walked to the window to see if Whitey's car had pulled away. No one ever forgot that, however silly Whitey's posturing made him look, the prick was deadly and would kill — liked to kill — in a flash.

"Of course I do. He pays us money to operate," I jumped in. "In fact, Whitey hid at Hank's house at the Cape while I was hunting him."

"Well, listen to this one," Billy responded, as he sat back down inside our circle.

All the guys stopped what they were doing, all ears focused on Billy Sheehan. It might have been the booze and drugs kicking in, or it might have been the disdain in which these guys held Whitey Bulger that made this story come out.

"Hank told me that one night at Blinstrum's he was in the back room with Sal Mineo."

"Sal Mineo?!" Tommy interrupted. "The actor?"

Billy sneered. "No, Sal Mineo the astronaut! Of course I mean the actor!" Billy paused for a second and then continued. "I guess in the back of the nightclub there's an entertainment room for various unofficial stuff. Well, apparently old Whitey Bulger walked in on Sal sucking Hank's cock. What did Jimmy do? He dropped his drawers and fucked Sal in the ass."

There was a brief, stunned silence. Then whole place exploded with laughter one more time. I wanted to question it but the idea of Jimmy fucking Sal Mineo was just too comical. Gross, but comical. When I think about it now I wonder how this guy could ever have made it to the FBI's Most Wanted list.

Later that night Billy questioned me about why Jimmy would drive all the way down to the Cape just to sit in the driveway. Of course, just as he'd concealed his homosexuality, he was a master at hiding the truth. No one back then had any inclination that Whitey was the number-one informant for the FBI in New England. That was simply inconceivable. At that point no one knew about the FBI's Top Echelon Informant Program, in which the FBI targeted as informants not the usual lowlife drug dealers or midlevel hit men, but guys at the very top of the criminal ladder.

The Charlestown guys got all revved up when I told them Whitey wanted me to stop helping the IRA. These guys had a mischievous side that told them "If Whitey don't want it done, let's do it!" Also, the Townie guys had parents off the boat from Ireland, so it excited them to help the IRA, which everyone respected for its commitment and expertise.

When I think back on it now, that trip to Hyannis is when the *Valhalla* plan got started. For the rest of the evening and well into the next morning we did nothing but brainstorm ways to bring guns to the IRA. Roughly two years from that night, two guys sitting in that room, Jimmy Flynn and Baby Hughie, would cross the Atlantic Ocean as crewmen on the *Valhalla*. And with them was one of the largest shipments of arms ever smuggled for the IRA.

Everything really got underway after we returned to Boston. It's funny how success brings IRA men out of thin air. One day in 1983, I stopped by Peter Curran's house, on the corner of P Street and Fourth, just to check in and see how things were progressing. The next thing I knew I was face to face with an IRA volunteer named Sean Crawley. Sean, who was probably twenty-five at the time, looked like a choirboy with his short black hair and thin wire-rimmed glasses neatly tucked around his ears. Crawley wasn't that tall, but his compact, muscular build gave some indication of his background as a former Force Recon Marine. That fact alone was cause enough to consider him dangerous. The U.S. Marine Corps Force Recon teams are the equivalent of the Navy's SEALS. In fact, Force Recon preceded the SEALS. All Marines undergo rigorous training, but those who volunteer to become Force Recon Marines acquire the best training on the planet. They are scuba- and airborne-qualified and train with other special forces units, mostly the SEALS. Sean had completed the Navy's scuba- and underwater-assault tactics training. He'd learned how to jump with the Army Airborne and had Force Recon jungle training. Force Recon training doesn't stop; as long as you are a marine you are given the most advanced training in both weapons use and survival techniques. You can see why the IRA took in Crawley. Sean and I hit it off the moment we sat down in Curran's living room and started to reminisce about the Corps.

Things happened fast after we met. We found him a cot and he moved into my living room in my house on Broadway. Whitey didn't like it too much; I think he sensed Sean didn't respect him. And he was right. Sean was so focused and determined that he didn't have any time for Whitey's advice on how the IRA should conduct the war. What did Whitey, a disgraced Air Force dropout, know about urban guerilla warfare? Sean would listen politely, a slightly pained expression on his face, and then he'd find a reason to leave the room. Sean was such a quiet, easygoing guy; he had a great sense of humor and was very intelligent, and spent the majority of his free time reading history. It was a perfect union between us; we had our shared backgrounds of our Irish birth and the Marine Corps, further strengthened by our shared faith in a common cause.

I still cannot remember how it first came up, but one night we were sitting around my apartment talking about the weapons the IRA lacked. Sean talked about how poorly trained they were compared to the Brits. That was natural; after all, the IRA was fighting an empire. We both understood how important it was to have dependable weapons and the best training. The IRA knew all too well that, without proper training, even the most courageous volunteers could fail. As the Marine Corps rifle instructors drummed into us, "Bullets go where you aim them, not where you want them to go!" Sean wanted me to help train some of the IRA men in the use of the 106 recoilless rifles that I'd used in Vietnam. Sean also expressed interest in acquiring ammunition pouches, rifle stabilizers to make accurate shooting easier, ammo cans, waterproof rifle bags that would allow weapons to be hidden deep in the Irish bogs, and training manuals.

He was now talking about accessories, and it occured to me to enlist the help of *Shotgun News*. I always had copies of *Guns & Ammo*, *Soldier of Fortune*, and *Shotgun News* stacked in the bathroom and on the coffee table — all magazines dedicated to the legal sale of weapons and the latest news on the best weaponry available.

"Sean, check this out," I said, as I tossed him a copy of *Shotgun News*. "Everything you want — manuals, ammo boxes, all the accessories you need — can be bought by way of the U.S. mail."

Sean squinted as he looked at one page, flipped it, and looked at another. At the third page he chuckled and closed the magazine. It took the briefest moment to sink in, but then Sean smiled. "It's all here — all the extras we need!" He opened it up again and sat back in his chair in disbelief as each page presented him with things he needed to adequately equip efficient IRA volunteers.

"You gotta be jokin' me, Pat," he blurted out in a stronger-than-usual brogue.

"No, I'm dead serious. In fact, you can buy every piece of a machine gun right through that magazine."

"You can buy a machine gun?" he responded, incredulous.

"Well, not quite. You can't buy a machine gun, but you can buy every part of a machine gun except the firing mechanism."

Sean was suddenly quiet. I could hear him breathing. He sat back, adjusted his eyeglasses, and looked up at the ceiling as he began to think about the possibilities. All marines are trained to break down weapons, clean them, and put them back together. I could almost hear Sean assembling an M60 in his mind.

"Pat? Wait. You mean if we get a firing mechanism in Ireland we can build a .50 caliber machine gun?"

"Sean, if you can get firing mechanisms you can build any rifle or any weapon on the market. The firing mechanism is what makes all the difference," I added — foolishly, I realized after I'd said it, because Sean knew that better than anyone. In Force Recon, Sean had handled just about every weapon on the planet.

"And you can buy all the parts right here?" he asked, as he held up the copy of *Shotgun News*.

I nodded.

"Why would they allow that? And why would there be a market for military machine guns in the States, Pat?"

"Think about it. Veteran groups like the American Legion buy the parts and build the weapon for the front of their halls. I've actually seen .50 caliber machine guns displayed around military monuments in the center of towns. They're the real things — without a firing mechanism. And with a lot of paint on them."

Sean had the unbridled enthusiasm of an unsupervised child in a candy store. Over the next few days he spent all his time sitting on the edge of the cot circling classified ads in the back of *Shotgun News*. I don't think he truly believed me. Every night I'd come home and Sean would immediately fling open *Shotgun News* and point to weapons parts. "Do you think we can get this, Pat? How about these, Pat, can we buy ammunition for rifles like this says?"

Sean was floored when I informed him that in some states you needed absolutely nothing, not even a license, to purchase live ammunition.

"Sean, buying weapon parts, ammunition, and manuals are the easy part. I can use an alias and get the stuff sent to the yacht club. No one will be able to trace the purchases." I had finally broken his trance. He looked up at me. "But first, before we order one round of ammunition, we have to find a way to get everything safely to Ireland."

Sean nodded; he knew we'd need a delivery system bigger than vans and furniture containers. That's when I brought Whitey into the equation. I thought I had no choice there, but thinking back on it, that was a big mistake.

Early one Sunday morning Sean and I met Whitey and Kevin Weeks in Southie and they followed us over to Peter Curran's house. Sean and I put all the cards on the table. We had done our research thoroughly, and Peter was jacked up to see it all go down. I watched Whitey gradually warm to the idea, but I'm sure he was trying to find something in the plan for him.

"Pat, what address are you going to use for shipping the weapon parts?" Whitey asked.

"The Columbia Yacht Club. I've got an Irish guy who will sign for it. They'll just leave it there for me to pick up."

"Have you thought about the heat this will bring to Southie, Pat?"

"We aren't doing anything illegal. Nowhere in America is it against the law to buy ammunition, gun parts, and manuals to store," I countered.

"But we break the law the day they move to Ireland," Whitey responded. "That's gunrunning." But he didn't say that in a negative way; instead, his voice crackled with excitement. He seemed to come alive at the prospect. Whitey loved reading about military history. He was such a pompous asshole; I think he was imagining himself as a brilliant military-campaign strategist and international gunrunner for the IRA. And that was big enough to satisfy even *his* ego.

"If you want to smuggle that amount of weapons we need to go to one of the major drug dealers," Whitey said as he nodded his head, as if he had now taken charge. But he was right. Joe Murray was the major dealer in Boston. He lived in Charlestown. I'd met Joe Murray on a few occasions: weddings, fundraisers, political rallies. I wasn't aware of it then, but Joe paid Whitey to operate his drug-smuggling business safely. "Safely" meant that Whitey wouldn't kill you. This is just another example of how we didn't know everything Whitey was up to.

Joe Murray was 6'4" with light blonde hair, thirty-eight years old and full of himself. He loved taking risks when large sums of money were on the line. He had been very successful at smuggling marijuana from the Florida Keys into Gloucester, Massachusetts. But the plan we were concocting was quite different; we needed a boat to cross the Atlantic. Sailing up the East Coast was one thing — the Atlantic Ocean was another.

I called a meeting one night with Joe Murray, Whitey, Sean, and the boys from Charlestown. We all met at Joe's house across from the Bunker Hill Projects. "We have a deal for you," Whitey said. Joe never balked; all he wanted was more detail. It was a "soft shakedown," and Joe started to warm up immediately.

I could tell Sean didn't like Joe much, but he kept it hidden. Murray was a good enough guy but he was arrogant. He had a lot of liquid assets at his disposal, and that made him look down on people. His attitude was that he was indispensable — and in this case, as long as he had the money and the boat, he was. Sean knew Joe would be useful, so his personal feelings had to be put aside.

To ensure Joe's commitment, Sean filled Murray's head with facts about Northern Ireland, and over the next few months Joe read all the Irish history books I could get him. It was hard not to believe in the Republican cause if you were an Irish American; it was almost impossible to not become emotionally attached and involved. All Sean and I had to do to convince Joe was lay out the facts.

Joe Murray finally came to me one day and said, "We can do this, Pat. We can do this!"

"This" was the biggest thing we, or anyone else, had done for the IRA. That moment was the birth of the *Valhalla*.

16. SEVEN TONS OF GUNS

Joe Murray had successfully smuggled marijuana up and down the East Coast for roughly four years, from 1979 to 1983. He owned several boats that allowed his operation to move undetected through the waterways from Maine to Florida. But one thing he lacked was a boat big enough and strong enough to cross the Atlantic with seven tons of weapons, which was what we needed. Well, to be accurate, we had no idea then that what we loaded onto the boat would be seven tons of weapons; we simply knew it would be more than a Boston Whaler could move!

In March 1984, Brendan Kelly, a front man for Joe Murray, purchased the *Surge*, a 120-foot steel fishing vessel, with the sole intention of crossing the Atlantic with our weapons load; there would be no marijuana on board. We wanted nothing to do with that on this shipment. A man named Clayton Smith, who had captained boats for Joe in several of his previous drug-smuggling operations, was thought to be quite capable of navigating the Atlantic crossing, and we tapped him to pilot the *Surge*.

There was one problem: Smith informed Murray that the *Surge* was not quite ready. But Murray was not going to allow anything to stop him. He was now committed to the IRA's fight. It was hard not to be, given the conditions in Northern Ireland and the policies of the United States government that allowed the repressions to continue. Anybody who cared about the Irish understood it was time to take charge, to rewrite the rules of engagement. I'd convinced Joe that what we were doing was not only right but necessary. I think what Joe's life had lacked until then was passion for something like the struggle for Irish freedom; he'd made lots of money, but that wasn't enough to give his life meaning. Joe really embraced his role as an IRA supporter; it made him feel good to contribute to something as noble as helping the Irish get the Brits out of their — and his— ancestral home. And Joe put his money where his passion was.

Murray didn't flinch when Smith gave him this news, and handed over two cash payments of $1,500 each. The *Surge* was moved from Rockland, Maine, to a boatyard in South Boston and the repairs began. Joe had a young marine mechanic by the name of John McIntyre who'd worked the engine room on all the marijuana runs. He was a rugged-looking kid with a brilliant ability to keep an engine going at sea. But he drank, and now, when he was drunk, he began telling everybody he had been indoctrinated into the IRA and was on a special mission. He had the passion we looked for, but the way he went overboard when he drank was troubling. Obviously the IRA and its supporters prized secrecy — otherwise you risked capture, incarceration, maybe execution. That was our reality. But McIntyre wasn't a criminal at our level. Sure, he was smuggling weed with Joe, but that was nothing compared to what we'd been doing.

Both of McIntyre's parents had been spies for the United States during the Cold War. The kid knew a lot of influential people but had disgraced his parents the day he got booted out of the U.S. Army on drug charges. Sean thought it was funny, McIntyre actually believing he was now an IRA foot soldier. I told Joe that McIntyre was bad medicine. But Murray trusted McIntyre, said he was the guy with balls enough to cross the Atlantic. I left it alone because somebody had to keep the boat running; and the guys I was going to bring on board as additional crew from Charlestown had never even been to sea. I had to leave the McIntyre decision up to Sean — the IRA guy running the show; after all, he was going to be on the boat to make sure the weapons got to the transfer point.

After about three months of doing repairs McIntyre informed

Joe that the *Surge* wasn't going to make it. And, in a further com-
plication, several days later Clayton Smith was hospitalized in
Boston and needed major surgery. But Joe didn't miss a beat. He
was cool under pressure — that's what I liked about him. Murray
told Sean and me that a guy from Gloucester was the person we
needed to make the Atlantic run. Captain Bob Andersen, then
forty-five, had tremendous experience fishing the Grand Banks for
swordfish. Joe said Andersen had maneuvered through storms at
sea that would have shipwrecked most.

Andersen had also pled guilty in 1981 to violating U.S. laws reg-
ulating commercial fishing. He'd been caught smuggling $84,000
worth of Canadian swordfish into the States. The U.S. marshals
had seized the *Kristen Lee*, Andersen's 77-foot trawler, given him
a one-year suspended sentence, placed him on probation, and
forced him to pay several thousand dollars in fines.

This may sound cliché but, in gunrunning, timing is everything.
We had two things in our favor: Andersen needed a job and a boat,
and we needed a seaworthy boat and a captain with balls.

In June 1984 the *Kristen Lee* was purchased in Boston at a U.S.
marshal's auction by Leeward, Incorporated. That morning Bob
Andersen stood in the crowd giving instructions to Leland Schoen,
a strawman for Andersen and Leeward. Immediately the corporation hired Andersen to captain the fishing vessel. (Joe Murray was
the corporation.) Andersen changed the boat's name to *Valhalla* in
honor of his Danish ancestry. According to the Norse myth,
Valhalla was the final resting ground of fallen warriors.

Now all we needed was a large supply of weapons.

In April 1984 Joe Murray asked us if we could have all the
weapons by September. From that point forward, acquiring the
weapons became a full-time job for Sean and me. Our bank on Old
Colony Avenue, as well as the Columbia Yacht Club, was beginning
to see a lot more of my alias, Patrick Mullen. When I think back on
it now it was just pure coincidence that the bank, the name of

which I can't recall, didn't have camera surveillance at the teller windows. Sean and I thought it was a score back then, but we failed to anticipate that the money orders we were purchasing were totally traceable. And of course they were.

Most of the weapons were sent to the Columbia Yacht Club on 1825 Columbia Road in South Boston. It was a small, members-only club. And it was quiet; it seemed nobody was ever there except the custodian, and he was only there from 9 to 5. All the members would be out in their boats. I'd been a member of the yacht club since the early seventies, when I'd bought my first small sailboat. Whitey Bulger was also a member, along with his brother, state senate president William Bulger.

Most of the packages came addressed to Patrick Mullen; although nobody would ever admit to it, the members knew Patrick Mullen was me. The custodian was a good old guy. I told him never to sign his own name; I told him to alternate between Arthur Brown and Michael Jones. The UPS guys never looked at the signature. They were pushed for timely deliveries, and these boxes weighed between twenty-five and fifty pounds — they had no intention of carrying them back to their trucks.

It's amazing — and most people I tell cannot for a moment believe it — but we assembled the majority of the *Valhalla*'s cargo through ads in *Shotgun News*. Sean would circle the ad and write the quantity he wanted beside it. I'd call the 800-number, give the voice on the other end of the line my order and the Columbia Yacht Club's mailing address, call Joe Murray for cash, hit the bank for a money order, and then head to the post office to send it off. Ten days after placing our first order cargo for the *Valhalla* began to arrive in boxes. It was just that simple. There was nothing to it — in fact, my days felt boring. But Sean loved the business of acquiring our stash. His favorite line became "America — what a country!" I think that Sean was so immersed in the struggle for Ireland that he'd forgotten he was also American.

In the first week of April 1984 we purchased ammunition cans from Jolly Roger in Roxbury, Pennsylvania, for close to $400 and weapons-training manuals from both Sierra Supply Company in Durango, Colorado, and Amherst Arms in Laurel, Maryland. It was very important to properly train soldiers on the cleaning, handling, and firing of their weapons. You don't just buy guns and give them to soldiers. That's why Marine Corps training is the best in the world — every marine knows not just how to handle and fire a weapon but also how to keep it clean so that it's ready when you need it. That rifle prayer in *Full Metal Jacket*? Yes, we did that. We were taught to revere our rifles, because in combat your rifle is your life.

At first we kept the orders inexpensive and not very risky. We were testing the waters to see if anybody monitored our purchases — buying weapons this way seemed almost too easy to be true!

On April 6, 1984, Sean had highlighted a classified ad in *Shotgun News* placed by Numrich Arms Company out of West Hurley, New York, for nylon rifle clips, rifle covers, and .50 caliber side-mount ammunition. I spoke to the owner at length that day. He was very amenable. It's a funny thing — if you speak as though you have a right to what you're doing and you speak with authority, hardly anyone will question you. I ordered one thousand M16 machine gun magazines, one hundred rifle covers, 120 eight-ounce cans of rifle-board cleaner, fifty side-mounting ammo cans for .50 caliber machine guns, and one MT Linker for linking machine gun belts together.

I specified that the M16 magazines be nylon, not aluminum, and I thought the owner might pause. He didn't. The magazines are usually aluminum and are approximately half the price of nylon magazines, but nylon magazines are corrosion resistant and a little more impact resilient. The Israelis use them and the Canadian army has recently switched from aluminum to nylon. The marines have used nylon magazines for quite some time.

The IRA hid a lot of their weapons in the bogs that make up most of Ireland's countryside. Therefore, it was very important that we purchase rifle bags of an appropriate size to protect the weapons from water. You can't just throw weapons in a duffle bag and bury them in a bog. You need bags treated with special chemicals to protect the firing mechanism. The rifle bags I ordered were forty-eight inches long and tied off at the end; they are the guarantee that your weapon won't rust while it's submerged in peat.

The total order from Numrich Arms came to around seven grand. The owner, a man named Phil Hunter, asked for a cashier's check for half that amount, and I mailed it on the following day. On April 12, Joe Murray and I drove in Joe's black Blazer to rural upstate New York to pick up our order. There was a slight risk, of course, that if Hunter became suspicious he might trigger surveillance, endangering our mission. But we weren't really concerned about getting caught. It wasn't that Joe and I were cocky, it's just that we were doing nothing illegal. According to federal law, there's only one part of a gun — the part known as the framer receiver — that is illegal to purchase as a stand-alone item. It was illegal to purchase the framer receiver in 1984 and it still is illegal. You can buy every other part of a gun in New York — back then you didn't even need to show a driver's license to complete the sale.

Numrich was set up like any military surplus facility. The majority of Numrich's business was mail order, so their retail store was very small. Phil Hunter was of medium build, about forty years old, and only the hair just above his ears was silver-gray. Hunter took Joe and me into his office and we exchanged formalities. Because I had established our relationship, Joe left me to do all the talking. We didn't stay more than twenty minutes — it was all business. Joe carried the boxes to the Blazer as Hunter and I went over the purchase order. I handed over $3,500 in cash and

Joe and I headed back to Southie with boxes stuffed into every available space in that Blazer.

Later in April, feeling that everything was going smoothly, we went ahead and made our first big purchase: three rocket warheads from Barnicle Wharf Trading Company in Newark, New Jersey.

From April to August 1984 we purchased more than $500,000 worth of weapons parts, manuals, and miscellaneous military accessories using *Shotgun News* classified ads, a telephone, a bank, the post office, the United Parcel Service, and the Columbia Yacht Club. No one asked questions, no one stopped us, and it was all perfectly legal. Amazingly, the easiest purchase was the antiaircraft weapons.

We were able to buy every single part to an antiaircraft weapon through mail order. Using our Marine Corps training, and referring to other manuals, Sean and I cleaned the weapons. The middle of the barrel was soldered together but we didn't care. The IRA had machines to billow them out or remove the solder once in Ireland.

The closest we ever came to anyone becoming suspicious was in mid-June. Numrich's main mail-order competitor in *Shotgun News* was Sarco, a company located in Sterling, New Jersey. Sean had found a sale and I'd ordered $20,000 worth of weapon parts for both .50 caliber and .30 caliber machine guns, one thousand rounds of .50 caliber ammunition, 150 HK91 magazines, and ten cases — twenty thousand rounds — of 9mm ammunition. They asked for a money order for three grand.

On June 29, Joe, Sean, Mick Murray (no relation to Joe), and I drove the Blazer and a Dodge van to rural Sterling to pick up the order. Charles Steen, the owner, was a short, balding man in his late fifties. His family had run the business for almost thirty years. The warehouse was stocked with standard military surplus, everything boxed on large shelves in perfect order. Steen's suit coat was wrinkled, and he looked a little tense. I'm sure that the amount of the order, coupled with the likes of Joe, Sean, Mick, and me, made him a bit suspicious. Sean and Mick pulled the vehicles around to the back of the warehouse while Joe and I followed Steen to his office.

"Large order," Steen remarked. "What are you guys going to do with all this?"

"It's for our yacht club members," Joe replied.

I squirmed a little and shot a disapproving eye toward Joe. He should have let me do the talking, and by the look on his face he understood that. Mr. Steen was now searching his desktop for our invoice.

"Machine gun rounds for your yacht club?"

"It is more of a game club that happens to be right on the water," I replied. "We're all Vietnam vets, so we're still into gun collecting."

Steen located our invoice file and then caught my eye. I could see him trying to size me up.

"We take our members up to New Hampshire every week to shoot at some ranges. The machine gun parts are a collector's item for conversation around our club. We sell them, too."

He seemed to buy it — especially when I handed him a small gym bag with $17,000 in cash. Joe and I followed him into the warehouse, where Sean and Mick were waiting to load the merchandise. Steen directed us to the boxes of ammunition. Sean and Mick began to load the cases into the van, and I watched as he counted the money.

"Oh," Steen spoke up, "about the nine-millimeter cases. I'm going to need a copy of a driver's license."

Everybody stopped.

"Sean," I jumped in, "do have your license on you?"

Sean dug into his wallet and politely walked it over to Steen. For what seemed like several minutes Steen turned it over and over, making his inspection.

"An Arizona license, Massachusetts plates, and the Columbia Yacht Club in South Boston? I'm afraid this isn't going to do," he finally said. "I need a license from Massachusetts." Steen gulped. He was in a tough spot and he knew it. He didn't want to piss off these hard-looking guys lurking around his store, but he didn't want to get caught in legal trouble either.

"Forget about it," I replied without making a fuss. "Just deduct that from our order."

He froze for an instant, but after a moment he didn't seem too concerned. Just then I saw a sign for a sale on AK-47 rounds. I knew that the sign would save us. In the state of New Jersey you can buy machine gun rounds without a license. But 9mm rounds are for handguns and are thus controlled by the federal government.

"Hey, why don't you make up the difference in those AK-47 rounds on sale," I asked.

"Sure, but I'll need a copy of your tax identification to finalize the order in our records."

I nodded and handed him a copy of a fake tax identification number for the Columbia Yacht Club. Twenty minutes later I jumped into Joe's Blazer. We stopped on the turnpike for coffee and something to eat. All of us were quiet. Sean sensed that we had just come very close to jeopardizing his trip back to Ireland with the weapons we'd spent the last four months collecting.

The stuff we couldn't buy from *Shotgun News* we got the old-fashioned way — the way the Mullen gang had become notorious for. We stole it. Handguns, hunting rifles, and shotguns filtered through South Boston on a regular basis. Instead of Whitey using them (to kill someone) or selling them, we'd confiscate them for the cause. At first Whitey didn't seem to mind. But suddenly he started to complain. In fact, about six months into it he asked me to get out, to quit the operation. He thought it was consuming too much of my time. I refused. He knew I'd never give up, so he let it go after one outburst.

In all Joe Murray paid more than one million dollars to buy seven tons of weapons; two fishing boats, the *Surge* and the *Valhalla*; plane tickets; and ten hunting/sniper rifles he purchased legally using his real Massachusetts driver's license at several local licensed gun dealers around the Boston area.

I contributed a few dollars by hitting up every drug dealer and bookie I knew. I figured it was like making a political contribution. I'd sit down with the dealer or bookie and a few of my guys, we'd talk about the size and take of the dealer's or bookie's operation, and then I'd tell him how much his contribution was going to be. It was easy. Most times we even got a little more.

Sean and I traveled from Boston to New York to Pittsburgh and visited with every IRA soldier in between. A group in Philadelphia gave us twenty-five mini-14 machine guns; another organization found us cases of hand grenades. One IRA guy from New York traveled to South Boston by train with a duffel bag containing twelve pump shotguns. We met him at Braintree Station and he was back in New York the same day.

The weapons were stored in several safe houses throughout central Maine and New Hampshire, the bulk of it packed in the basements of summer and winter vacation homes belonging to Joe Murray. By September the time had come: Captain Bob Andersen was ready, we had a crew, and Sean's mission in South Boston was nearly complete. One week before the *Valhalla* sailed Joe rented two U-Haul vans and moved the weapons to homes around Boston, to individuals we could trust to say nothing, people whose hearts were connected to Northern Ireland and Northern Aid. The night before the *Valhalla* sailed, Sean and Mick Murray wiped down all the guns and drill-pressed all the serial numbers on the magazine welds to eliminate any traceable records.

On September 13, right after dusk, Sean and I moved all the

weapons from the safe houses to Gloucester Harbor. Captain Bob Andersen, John McIntyre, Jimmy Flynn, and Baby Hughie worked extremely fast to load the boxes on board the *Valhalla*. It took us the whole night to complete the task. Whitey, Kevin, and Stevie Flemmi watched from an adjacent pier to make sure nobody had seen us carrying the cargo onboard. We paid the crew nothing: each one of them agreed to volunteer because they believed in the IRA cause. The *Valhalla* was now ready.

The toughest part of the departure was saying goodbye to Sean. He'd lived with me, and we'd had so many laughs. But we were both soldiers on a mission, and his was always a more serious — and deadly — mission. If we were to ever meet again we would conduct business right where we left off. As we shook each other's hands and hugged — and I'm not much of a hugger — we took pride in what we'd accomplished. Both of us knew there was a chance we'd never see each other again. That was the nature of the game, and we accepted it. But I'll tell you, when you face death or imprisonment for the things you do because you believe in what you're doing, you appreciate the time you spend with your comrades of the same spirit, men like Sean Crawley.

17. THE ATLANTIC OCEAN

Sean Crawley said we lucked out when Clayton Smith had to back out of captaining the *Surge*. Bob Andersen not only brought to the job a boat much more capable of crossing the treacherous Atlantic but, even better, he hated the British. Andersen, Irish American as well as Danish, had long been an IRA sympathizer and a contributor to NORAID-sponsored events. Bob held a master's degree from Wentworth Institute of Technology in Boston and was well read on the history of atrocities the Brits had committed in Northern Ireland.

John McIntyre finished a complete check of the *Valhalla's* mechanical operating system late on Sunday evening. At 12:03 A.M. on September 14, 1984, Captain Bob maneuvered out of Gloucester Harbor with a crew that included John McIntyre, Sean Crawley, Baby Hughie, and Jimmy Flynn. Besides Andersen, only John McIntyre knew anything about being at sea.

Fall was in the air and the moon's bright glow bounced off the water. I watched Sean signal me a final wave before the *Valhalla* cut a hard left toward the open sea.

Andersen had estimated that it would be twelve days before they could hand off the weapons to the IRA. I'd never thought about the *Valhalla* getting caught with the weapons. But I couldn't help but wonder if they would cross the Atlantic safely.

Andersen had disguised the trip perfectly. He had twenty tons of ice loaded below, one hundred pounds of squid and seven thousand pounds of mackerel for bait, and thirty miles of long-line fishing gear on an eight-foot spool. Other than the seven tons of weapons neatly packed inside the forward engine room, the

Valhalla easily passed for being on a routine swordfish excursion to the Grand Banks.

The first day out Andersen ordered McIntyre to lay the boat to, to rest or drift. They had run up against a small hurricane just south of Nova Scotia, near Seal Island. From the northeast the seas quickly grew to twelve to fifteen feet, pummeling the *Valhalla*. Water was starting to trickle into the forward cabin and compromise the weapons. Andersen suggested the crew move all seven tons of weapons to higher ground for safety. Sean Crawley led the crew, and in a little more than three hours they walked each box of weapons to a designated dry area in the middle of the *Valhalla's* top deck. Andersen decided it was a waste of energy to fight the sea, so he drifted for fourteen hours.

Finally the seas subsided enough for Andersen to give the go-ahead to McIntyre to power up. Sean, Flynn, and Baby Hughie spent another three or four hours carrying everything back down to the forward engine room, where they once again neatly repacked everything.

On the third night the trip almost came to an abrupt end. They had just entered the treacherous waters off Sable Island, called the "graveyard of the Atlantic" because of the 350 recorded ship-wrecks scattered off its beaches. Andersen and McIntyre had been spelling each other for six-hour shifts at the wheel. Andersen had just taken over in the pilothouse when he noticed something on the radar screen. For sixty minutes Bob monitored the other ship's course. He had a gut feeling things were off. McIntyre began monitoring channel 16 on the ship's VHF radio, and they watched, waiting for anything that seemed out of the ordinary.

Most of the crew was sleeping, but as the large vessel on the radar began to gain ground on the *Valhalla*, Andersen ordered McIntyre to wake up Crawley. Sean immediately went to the pilot-house and Bob showed him a tiny dot on the Valhalla's radar. Bob had determined that the ship that had been following the *Valhalla* for almost an hour was a Canadian naval vessel patrolling their waters; he told Crawley that a fishing vessel would not set its coordinates directly at the *Valhalla*. He was not positive it was a Canadian naval vessel, but since it came from Halifax in a straight line toward the *Valhalla*, it was a pretty safe bet.

Andersen had failed to register with the Canadian authorities. He made a judgment call and decided to take his chances, thought he'd have a chance at downplaying his failure to register if they called him on the *Valhalla's* radio.

"What are we gonna do?" Crawley asked, concerned.

"I think the jig is up, Sean. I'll monitor channel 16 for a while, but I think we have to dump the weapons into the Atlantic."

The Canadian navy had been watching the *Valhalla* from a safe distance of three miles. Bob advised Crawley to wake up the crew and carry all the weapons to the deck. "If they close under three miles, Sean, we'll have to toss 'em." Sean didn't balk. Flynn, Baby Hughie, McIntyre, and Sean got everything topside in double time; at this point they didn't have three hours to move the cargo.

Andersen was cool; he never panicked. Of course, Sean was trained for situations in which split-second decisions had to be made, so a sense of confidence came over the crew. As soon as the guns were covered and out of plain sight, Andersen lit up the ship. He figured an eighty-seven-foot ship completely illuminated would obviously not be trying to conceal anything illegal. About the same time the northeast winds began to kick up the sea, the waves slamming forcefully against the *Valhalla's* steel hull. Already behind schedule, Andersen went a step further with the Canadian navy observers. He decided to slow down, cut engine power, and act like a swordfishing boat.

The Canadian naval vessel followed them closely for another two hours. Bob monitored the radio, waiting for some type of call. Sean sat below quietly with the crew, ready for the signal to dump the weapons. But the word never came. At about three in the morning, just east of Newfoundland off the Flemish Cap, the Canadian navy decided to turn and take another course. Andersen waited for almost an hour before making his move. He never became emotional; he just told McIntyre to have Sean and the boys repack everything back downstairs in the forward engine room.

For the next twenty-four hours the *Valhalla* had no problems in the waters of the mid-Atlantic. Andersen and McIntyre took turns at the wheel every six hours again, each checking the ship's GPS to ensure their course was aiming them toward the scheduled rendezvous off Porcupine Bank. Flynn cooked the meals, and there was no drinking — no alcohol had been allowed. On the fifth and sixth days the boat made good progress: almost 10 knots per hour, an average of 225 nautical miles per day. Most of the guys read or held political discussions about the IRA. Breakfast was usually between 7 and 8 A.M., lunch could be at noon or even as late as 2, and supper was always after 7.

The seventh day, September 20, was the day the sea almost swallowed the *Valhalla*. Andersen had heard about the hurricane before he'd left Gloucester. It was in the Bahamas, and there was no indication that it would turn and run north. But hurricanes do what they want; the winds began to intensify from the southeast. The sides of the *Valhalla* began to get hammered. One by one the crew became seasick.

At 5 A.M., McIntyre called Andersen up from below. The sea was beginning to swell and toss the ship around like a paper sailboat. At 6 A.M. Andersen took over. The pilothouse was 18 feet by 6 feet, three feet off the main deck, with seven windows wrapping around the front and sides to keep out the rain. But there was no rain — there was only wind and sea.

"What do you wanna do, Bob?" McIntyre asked.

"I'm not going to drift and be at the mercy of the sea. Cut power to six knots but maintain headway. We have to fight to keep the sea on her bow."

"The wind's too strong, Bob. I don't think I can maintain six knots."

Sean made his way to the pilothouse to see if he could help Andersen and McIntyre. He looked sick but had the courage to get out of his bunk.

"Water's trickling below," offered Sean. "If the charges get wet, we don't have to worry a bit about this sea."

"If we get a wave broadside, we're sunk and all bets are off. We'll push the bow right at the sea and take our chances."

Fifteen minutes later, just after McIntyre and Sean dropped below to tend to the engine room, the *Valhalla* slid down the side of a forty-foot wave and began to spin northwest. Bob said the wave came out of nowhere. It looked to be seventy feet high but was probably only forty or fifty feet. But Bob knew that twenty or thirty feet, give or take, didn't matter in this situation; he understood immediately that this wave was going to swamp them. He barely had time to get on his knees, hold the wheel steady, and duck under the steering house.

In just seconds the entire world changed for the *Valhalla* crew. Four of the seven pilothouse windows imploded. Water poured over the main deck and rushed below. Andersen was badly cut. Blood began rushing out of two large gashes on his right hand. The entire top deck was full of water, and the churning ocean was just getting warmed up.

For the next eight hours, into the early afternoon of September 20, Bob Andersen stood and guided the *Valhalla* directly into the walls of a sea trying to end the mission. McIntyre retrieved black electrical tape from the engine room and used it to stop the blood flowing from Andersen's right hand. The water streaming into the engine room had disabled the 110-volt generator, which knocked out the navigational system and cut the serial electricity. By this point the hurricane had moved and the wind was coming from the east-northeast. Bob was happy just to have the *Valhalla* upright and decided that his best chance of staying afloat lay in turning west, back toward Newfoundland.

Andersen had spoken privately with McIntyre about heading back to the States. He secretly felt the *Valhalla* could not withstand anymore. This was the dead center of hurricane season. Bob had warned Joe Murray that September was not the time to take the *Valhalla* across the Atlantic. He'd pleaded with Joe to wait until June 1985, saying that the westerly winds of September would make it very difficult to return home. "Joe, the *Valhalla* is a eighty-seven-foot fishing boat, not an ocean liner," Bob reasoned. But Joe told him they were sitting on a powder keg, and the IRA needed the weapons immediately.

Sean rallied the crew to the main deck to assist Andersen and McIntyre. In spite of the grave peril the crew was facing, Bob Andersen remained calm. In fact, he laughed out loud when he turned and saw Flynn, Baby Hughie, and Sean standing on deck, waiting for direction in full survival gear. "Shit," he joked, "take those off. If we go under the weight of those rubber suits will sink you. Or else they'll keep you afloat, so you can freeze to death for a few minutes longer."

Bob knew that if the *Valhalla* survived the day it would need immediate repair. Once the weather eased, he planned to turn the vessel east, pressing on toward Ireland even though McIntyre pleaded with him to head to Newfoundland for medical treatment and repair. But Bob didn't even consider that an option. He was fully aware of maritime law: The instant the *Valhalla* grounded on foreign soil — in this case, Newfoundland — the authorities would search the entire ship and cross-check the entire crew for criminal backgrounds. Andersen had no intention of throwing seven tons of weapons into the sea for a cut and four broken windows.

When the sea had begun to subside enough to maintain 6 knots, Bob ordered the men below to remove plywood from the bunks in the engineer's quarters in order to patch the four windows in the pilothouse. If the *Valhalla* was to continue toward Ireland, the pilothouse had to be secure, dry, and capable of withstanding any further onslaught. But the plywood wasn't flexible; it wouldn't bend to fit the curved steel windowsills of the pilothouse. Andersen remained cool and collected. He ordered McIntyre to incorporate blankets and mattresses as manmade gaskets. They wedged them into the open spaces between the plywood and steel to block any seawater. Sean and the boys worked for four hours before they fully secured the pilothouse and Andersen felt assured enough to turn the Valhalla back on an eastward track toward Porcupine Bank.

The next morning the sun seemed to lift the ocean. It had never been so calm; it looked like rolling blacktop stretching as far and as wide as the eye could see. McIntyre had worked through the night to get the generator and electricity back into full operation. The guys brought chairs out on deck and told their individual tales of survival. A few of the guys talked with Sean about the possibilities of going ashore in Ireland. Some of them wanted to actually stay and fight the British.

From late in the evening September 21 through early in the morning of September 27, the days were pretty much the same — nothing but a clear go and an unusually flat sea. Sometime around September 24, Bob Andersen had the *Valhalla* approximately six hundred miles off the coast of Ireland. The *Valhalla* was averaging 10 knots; the guys did a lot of reading, sleeping, and eating. Andersen and McIntyre spent most of the time talking about the return trip and how much money they could make off a catch of swordfish. Joe Murray had made a deal with Andersen; once he delivered the weapons, all the fish he could catch on the return voyage were his to keep for profit. Andersen knew a decent haul could bring him $100,000 back in Gloucester. They had both been to the Grand Banks before, and not many were better than Bob Andersen at finding schools of swordfish.

But on the morning of September 27, the fourteenth day at sea, a change came on fast. Andersen had just finished breakfast and was climbing the steps to the pilothouse when he spotted a plane in the eastern sky. Bob had seen many weather planes in his twenty-five years of fishing, but never one like this. He knew right away. This wasn't a weather plane. These guys were taking pictures.

"Everybody get below," Bob yelled. "Do not look up. Get below and don't come up until the plane has left the area."

"It's a weather plane, Bob," Sean watched as it passed. "It's a Royal Air Force weather plane. You'll see them out; it means we're getting close to England. Believe me, they are only checking the weather."

"Sean, we're in the soup! That guy is too low," Bob replied, as he watched it turn to make another pass over the *Valhalla*. "I've seen weather planes out here for more than twenty years — that is no weather plane."

On the night of the fourteenth day the *Valhalla* entered the waters known as Porcupine Bank, off the coast of Ireland. Andersen and the IRA had chosen this rendezvous location for two reasons. First, it was still in international waters — the *Valhalla* would not have to enter Irish waters and be subject to search. The second reason was simple — the *Valhalla* would not stand out here. Porcupine Bank is a fertile area well known to Irish fishermen. There were at least fifty fishing vessels in the general vicinity of the *Valhalla* on the night they arrived.

Shortly before midnight the *Marita Ann* broke the silence on a previously agreed upon VHF frequency. The *Marita Ann* had sailed out of Kerry with a crew of five, three of whom had no idea of their ultimate mission. Martin Ferris, the presumed IRA commander from Kerry, was on board, and he was the spokesman.

"You're two days late." The voice that cut over the *Valhalla*'s radio had a deep brogue.

"Late!" Andersen jumped in. "We just crossed the Atlantic Ocean in an eighty-seven-foot fishing vessel, ran headway into two small hurricanes, and had the Canadian navy trail us for hours."

Martin Ferris was not pleased that the *Marita Ann* had been idling at sea for the past two days. He understood that the longer his guys were aboard, the greater the risk of being caught. But Andersen was not the type of guy to shut his mouth when somebody criticized him, especially an individual who knew nothing about crossing the Atlantic. His rugged face and neck became crimson with anger. Sean Crawley heard what was going on and took over the radio inside the pilothouse. Crawley explained the situation to Ferris and everybody cooled off.

From that point on Martin Ferris, Sean Crawley, and Bob Andersen outlined plans to exchange the weapons at sea. Andersen knew they'd have to wait out another day, but he was exhausted and didn't have the energy to get into it with Martin Ferris at the moment. He knew Sean Crawley would understand the logic behind not moving seven tons of weapons in broad daylight.

Early the next morning, Jimmy Flynn fixed breakfast as Sean tried to contain his excitement. He'd spent more than a year of his life collecting and arranging the largest shipment of weapons ever to be brought to the IRA. But in his gut Andersen knew something just wasn't right. The Royal Air Force plane that had flown over their heads just one hundred yards above the ocean only served to amplify his prior concerns. Crawley entered the pilothouse behind Andersen and headed for the VHF. Bob watched as Sean checked the preselected band and prepared to call for the *Marita Ann's* position.

"Sean, I know you're not going to like this. And I know I said the exact same thing yesterday. But the jig is up."

"Is this about the plane?" Sean smiled.

"That plane was taking photographs of every commercial ship in the vicinity. Every fishing ship, including the *Valhalla*, has identifying markings, Sean. They are looking for us. We're in the soup!"

At first Sean laughed; he always got a kick out of Andersen's pet sayings. Sean also respected Andersen. He never questioned Andersen's intelligence or knowledge of the sea. However, Sean had come too far to consider any other options. Home was less than two hundred miles away, the weapons were secured, and the IRA was waiting less than thirty miles from their location. But Andersen was persistent.

"Sean, let's run for it. I know these waters — we can get back home and store them until spring."

"You don't understand. I can't tell Ferris we're heading back to America. You don't understand IRA ways."

"Throw them in the ocean. They got us. Let the IRA come drag the bottom. Sean, that plane was flying so low I could see the faces of the pilot and copilot."

Sean began to consider what Bob was saying. He was a soldier and knew that he had to follow orders. However, he had taken quite a liking to Andersen. Deep down inside he knew that Bob was probably right. Bob immediately recognized that Sean was at the very least pondering the situation.

"I'll bet you they've known all along that we were coming. In fact, that is probably why the Canadian navy vessel turned away — they were ordered to."

Sean just fastened his sight on the radio. He had no other options. At nine that morning Sean transmitted a request for location to Martin Ferris in the *Marita Ann*.

"Sean, we're all going to jail," Andersen whispered, "but I'm with you whatever happens."

Ferris didn't like it much when Andersen instructed him that the weapon transfer should wait until the cover of darkness. He put up a fight, but Captain Bob informed Sean he didn't even want to discuss it. Andersen figured that if the Royal Air Force was looking for the *Valhalla*, they'd never find it from the air against the black sea after sunset. Andersen told Sean to let Ferris know that "weather planes" don't fly at night; of course, Sean had no intention of angering Martin Ferris even more.

The *Valhalla* held a steady course; most of the crew sat reading all day, waiting for dark. In the early afternoon, as the wind came out of the northeast and the seas began to rise, John McIntyre began to worry about the weapons transfer. Bob Andersen still had a bad feeling and spent most of his time watching radar and looking toward the sky for low-flying planes. On the evening September 28, shortly after dusk, Flynn, Sean, and Baby Huey began carrying the weapons from the engine room to the top deck for the last time.

Sometime near 9 P.M. Sean contacted Martin Ferris over the VHF radio and gave instructions to line up the *Marita Ann* starboard to port against the *Valhalla*. The plan was for both ships to secure side by side and hand off the weapons. Between the two crews the process should have taken no longer than an hour. But at close to 10 P.M. the sea began to churn once again, with waves rising to ten feet and a strong wind coming up out of the west.

At this point the carefully orchestrated rendezvous began to fall apart. Water started to wash over the *Valhalla*'s deck, soaking the boxes of weapons. Ferris was not happy when planks from the *Marita Ann*'s wood hull snapped and splintered as the *Valhalla*'s steel hull slammed her with each angry wave. It was a joint decision to pull away and talk it over on the VHF radio. Andersen knew by then that the odds were very high that the RAF was monitoring all frequencies.

Andersen finally devised a ferry system whereby both ships would maintain position one hundred feet apart, a rope would be strung between each vessel, and the weapons would be shuttled from the *Valhalla* to the *Marita Ann* in a small dinghy. It was dangerous for several reasons, and John McIntyre became an instant hero when he volunteered to man the dinghy. Captain Bob thought he'd be the one chosen for the job because of his time at sea, but he was more than willing to let McIntyre take on the task.

Around 11 P.M. Sean Crawley and Jimmy Flynn started passing just enough weapons to McIntyre to fill the small dinghy but not sink it. McIntyre then began to move through the rough sea hand over hand along the rope. It was a worse than horrible scenario, but no reasonable alternatives were visible. It took fourteen trips to ferry the weapons from the *Valhalla* to the *Marita Ann* — fourteen trips hand over hand with wind gusts and seas that twice nearly filled the dinghy. Salt water drenched all the equipment and weapons. The wind gusts slowed McIntyre and nearly ripped his hands away from the snug rope on several occasions.

Finally, as daybreak was coming on, Sean Crawley said his good-byes to Jimmy Flynn, Baby Huey, and Captain Bob Andersen. He then climbed into the dinghy and became the last cargo McIntyre would transport that day. Finally, the seven tons of weapons were in the Irish Republican Army's possession.

Andersen immediately headed south toward the Azores to throw off any surveillance. He wholeheartedly believed they had been given up by an informant, but he also gave the *Valhalla* very good odds of outfoxing the RAF. After six hours spent heading in a southward direction without seeing or hearing any planes, Andersen was satisfied that nobody had followed him. He swung the *Valhalla* about for the Flemish Cap, off the Grand Banks.

Since none of the *Valhalla*'s crew was paid, the chance to make a score by catching swordfish was something they all were eager to do. They never quite made it to the Flemish Cap. For more than three days, fifty mile an hour winds kicked the *Valhalla* around the ocean. Flynn and Baby Huey became so violently ill they couldn't leave their bunks. Andersen and McIntyre talked it over and decided they just couldn't go it alone. At first they thought the sea would calm itself, but the conditions weren't like the two hurricanes they'd already encountered. The ride up and down four- to seven-foot waves was like spending three days on a small roller coaster.

Andersen thought it would be best to point the *Valhalla* toward Boston. He suspected the authorities might be looking for them in Gloucester Harbor and determined that Pier 7 in Boston Harbor was the safest place to dock. Bob's plan was to get off the *Valhalla* long enough to ask questions and read the local newspapers.

The *Valhalla* docked on October 13, 1984, at eleven o'clock in the evening. The U.S. Coast Guard had been searching for the *Valhalla* all along the eastern seaboard.

18. CIRCLE OF GREEN

As Captain Bob and Sean Crawley were making their way across the ocean toward Porcupine Bank, tailed by the Canadian navy, Mary Nee and I flew out of New York City with Joe Murray and his wife, Sue, and Mick Murray and his girlfriend, Kelly. We arrived in Dublin a week before Captain Bob's estimated arrival at Porcupine Bank. The four of us stayed at a new posh hotel just outside downtown Dublin; from there an IRA soldier took Joe, Mick, and me to the Shelbourne Hotel in Dublin, where we received the bad news: none of us would be going to greet the *Marita Ann*. Joe was angry; he thought he should be allowed to go, given the considerable amount of energy we'd expended, not to mention the money he'd spent. Joe wasn't used to not calling the shots.

I, on the other hand, felt as though I'd done my job and it was over for now. I'd gotten the weapons on their way to the IRA. It was none of my business how the weapons came off the *Marita Ann*. I took my orders and didn't give it a second thought. Joe was acting like a spoiled rich kid who wanted to be involved in every aspect of the operation, but that was simply Joe's ego getting in the way of clear thinking. The way I saw it, the IRA volunteers unloading the weapons didn't need us gawking at them. Also, our presence in Ireland — and believe me, Americans stick out as Americans, even in Ireland — might risk alerting the Garda and compromising the whole mission. Sure, it would have been great to see those crates come off the *Marita Ann* after we'd seen them loaded onto the *Valhalla* an ocean away, but I understood why the IRA wouldn't allow that to happen.

Before I left the meeting at the Shelbourne I asked the IRA guys if they would take some boxes of goods I'd brought along that Captain Bob and McIntyre had requested for the return journey. They promised to do so, which helped me calm Joe down on our ride back to our Dublin hotel.

Joe and I split up in Dublin after that — I think he was disgusted at what he saw as an insult and just wanted out. Joe blamed his wife as the reason for his departure; she was three months pregnant and complaining of morning sickness. But Mick and I knew Joe felt slighted and wanted to go back to Boston. Joe told me he'd wait for us there. Mick and I tried to look as if the whole matter was unimportant — we didn't want to fuel Joe's indignation. Mick said we'd be along in a few days, just as soon as we got the word on the weapons arriving safely.

Mick, Kelly, Mary, and I decided to take a little R and R — to rent a car and cruise the Irish countryside. Restful and relaxing was not at all how it turned out to be, however. I'll never forget the instant it all went down. No matter how much time separates me from that moment in Irish history, I can still feel the surge of complete despair that ran over me at that moment. I know now what it means to be floored.

I remember the tense mental fog as we waited for news on the *Valhalla*. I was cranky, on edge — everything bothered me. I couldn't sit still. It had been almost five full days without word. We were driving along the road in Charlestown, County Mayo. Mary saw me fidgeting and switched on the radio. She was probably tired of my jittery nerves. Somehow she figured music might calm me down.

I think we'd only gone about ten minutes, listening to traditional Irish music, when the music was interrupted with breaking news. A female news reporter was giving details about an IRA fishing boat that had been fired upon and seized on thePorcupine Bank in the early morning hours. She said the Irish Naval Service had captured many IRA soldiers and confiscated what was believed to be the largest shipment of guns and ammunition in Ireland's history.

Time stood still. My heart froze. Mick stopped the car instantly and pulled close to the brush. My stomach soured and began to flip flop. My first thought was, "I've failed. All this time, all this work, and I've failed." Mary opened her mouth, eyes wide. She didn't know all the details, because we'd never spoken about the plan in her presence. But she wasn't stupid. She'd overheard things and could put bits of the puzzle together. I mean, here we are in Ireland with Joe Murray and Mick and now an IRA weapons shipment gets seized. Mary may have been wild, but she was very bright. Mick didn't say a thing. He understood the game.

"We gotta get out of Ireland," I whispered.

Mick nodded.

The news reporter continued, stating that the Irish police were looking for other IRA organizers believed to be in Ireland. We drove the rental car southwest and boarded a ferry at Rosslare Harbor for Le Havre, and from there we went on to Paris. Joe Murray had already returned safely to Charlestown with his wife. And now he was our only way out — he was the money man.

We know now that Sean O'Callaghan, a former IRA commander in Kerry, was in fact a "tout," an informer for British intelligence who, among other things, claimed responsibility for alerting authorities to the weapons shipment on the *Marita Ann*. He'd sold his soul; he'd been "turned" by the Brits, who had him dead to rights on murder charges. Naturally, like all other rats, he claimed that he had renounced violence and the IRA's use of it. It's funny how a stone-cold killer can "renounce" violence once his freedom is at risk. Why can't these rats simply be honest and say that they feared being incarcerated for what they'd once done with a clear mind, and were now willing to betray their comrades and their own true beliefs to avoid going to jail?

But at the time Mick and I had no idea what had gone wrong. Our only goal was to get the hell out of France.

I called Joe Murray and asked him to wire us money and arrange for four plane tickets back to the States. Joe told me the *Valhalla* had not been caught. He said that British and American intelligence knew there was another boat but had lost track of it somewhere along the Grand Banks. Our guys were safe. We might have lost the weapons, but only the *Marita Ann* and its crew had been caught. In war you have to look at the upside, because there is always a downside. But for an instant I thought, "Okay, at least the *Valhalla* made it. We can try it again."

I couldn't sleep that night. Sean Crawley had been caught and I was concerned for him. I knew what could happen to him once he was in British custody. British intelligence thought nothing of torturing IRA men to get the answers they wanted. They tortured IRA volunteers without hesitation.

I wondered if I'd ever see Sean again back in Southie, exchanging Marine Corps stories and making fun of Whitey. My mind raced backward to an incident in my apartment on a warm July night when the air outside felt like a nasty wet blanket. Whitey had just come to visit and Sean decided to toy with him.

"How is the project going, Sean?" Whitey asked.

Sean grinned and didn't need to look my way; he knew I was smirking. I knew what was about to happen.

"A little slow, Jimmy, a little slow." He paused to glance down at a recent issue of *Shotgun News*. "Do you have any suggestions, Jimmy?"

I waited for the load of bullshit Whitey was bound to spew. He always had these grandiose ideas about weapons and warfare.

"I can get you these fuses that attach to the fuselage of a jet plane. Timed. Set them for whatever you want, burn right through the bottom of the planes." Whitey looked proud as he gaged Sean's expression.

"Why would you want to do that, Jimmy?" Sean asked, without looking up.

"Just so they knew you could," Whitey said, with a look on his face like he'd just formulated the invasion of Normandy.

Silence flooded the room. I couldn't look up. Here sat a Force Recon Marine who has managed to elude British government agents for years being given advice by Jimmy Bulger, Air Force washout.

"Good idea Jimmy! Really good idea!" Sean said with sudden switch of enthusiasm.

About twenty minutes later Whitey stood and made his exit. Sean just looked at me shaking his head. "What a fuckin' idiot. Can you believe he volunteered flares that would burn up a fuselage? Is he for real, Pat?" Sean was an IRA volunteer who believed in fighting the British occupation of his country. Sean was intent on targeting British military units in Ireland and elsewhere — legitimate targets in war. He was not targeting civilians. Sean was a man of deep integrity, and it only took a short time of being around him before you saw that quality in him.

Mary, Mick, Kelly, and I landed at Logan Airport in Boston on September 29, 1984. As Mary and Kelly approached the custom lines I sensed trouble. Mary had wisely chosen a young, green-looking agent. The four of us handed our passports over and he entered the numbers into his computer. I glanced around, checking for surveillance cameras. They covered every square foot of the place. Suddenly the custom agent's eyes registered alarm. I tried to move about to see the screen but he turned it off quickly.

"What's the problem?" I asked.

His lips moved but nothing came out, he was that panicked. The light at his station started to flash, and within seconds several state police officers surrounded us. Mary wasn't scared. She'd been in danger often enough — it came with the territory. She was my girlfriend and she knew this shit would happen — frequently. Mary knew to remain calm and focused. Mick and Kelly were old pros at being interrogated by police, and I didn't even flinch. Actually, I was amused by the agent's ridiculous reaction. Who the hell did they think I was: Al Capone?

They took all four of us into separate rooms and interrogated us for a good two hours. I was asked over and over again to describe every step of our trip through Ireland and France.

"What's this?" A customs agent asked, holding up my shillelagh.

"Wood!"

"We have to x-ray this," he responded.

The guy really thought he had something. Ten minutes later he came back and I just smiled. They went through my bag item by item. When they opened my personal bag they smelled my shampoo, aftershave, and deodorant. Each time they put an item down I'd throw it in the garbage.

"What are you doing?" one of them asked.

"I don't know what kind of diseases you guys have. Who knows what's jumping out of your noses. I'm not using this stuff again."

They were pissed. But finally I told them to either arrest me or let me call my lawyer. An hour later I was sitting in my house on Broadway across from the M Street Park drinking a beer with Whitey Bulger. Whitey had heard the newsflash earlier in the day. He thought the whole thing could become a headache for Southie — meaning him — but he acted supportive.

Meanwhile Captain Bob, John McIntyre, and the crew were still on the *Valhalla* somewhere in the Atlantic. They had no idea things were unfolding so fast, and only a fool would try and contact them to let them know. Andersen and the others were on their own.

By the time the crew arrived in Boston Harbor on the night of October 13, they had all lost a substantial amount of weight. Joe Murray picked me up and we headed for the harbor. I was with a top IRA soldier who was hiding in Southie. We met Captain Bob and John McIntyre at the Quincy pier. Seeing the damage suffered by the steel hull of the *Valhalla*, I was sure the *Marita Ann* had been really banged up during the weapons transfer. Joe handed over $10,000 in twenties to have the hull fixed quickly. We knew the authorities would be looking for a fishing boat and any damage might give them reason for suspicion, a reason to look more closely at the so-called "crew." The Irish authorities had the *Marita Ann* in custody, and Joe knew that if the U.S. authorities saw the *Valhalla's* damage they could match them up.

McIntyre agreed to fix the boat quickly. Joe thanked Captain Bob and McIntyre, and we entered into cautious discussion — cautious because Andersen and McIntyre had just told us what they'd gone through — about the possibilities of trying it again.

Ten minutes after we left the pier, U.S. customs agents stormed the *Valhalla*. The Coast Guard pulled alongside, and Joe and I saw television helicopters hovering over our heads as we drove away. The exchange of the weapons from the *Valhalla* to the *Marita Ann* had not been seen, and there was no evidence of weapons on the *Valhalla*, so we felt comfortable — relatively speaking. The possibility of one of the *Valhalla's* crew cracking was a risk, but we did not think that likely. Aside from Captain Bob, Joe and I had picked a crew of solid IRA sympathizers, except for one: McIntyre. He had come along with Captain Bob, and although he had convinced us of his sincere desire to help the IRA, I always thought he was something of a loose cannon.

My fears about McIntyre were realized when Captain Bob told me that McIntyre had folded when the feds seized the *Valhalla*. They'd cornered Captain Bob and McIntyre inside the pilothouse. McIntyre couldn't stop shaking. From what I understand

Andersen tried to calm McIntyre down by telling him to keep it simple: they had been fishing — unsuccessfully, but that's what they had been doing. The feds were performing their usual act, threatening life in jail forever to intimidate Andersen and McIntyre and to try to get them talking. But Andersen looked right through them and said, "You're on the wrong boat, gentleman. We've been fishing for swordfish and ran smack into the middle of a hurricane. Don't let these guys scare you, John."

They were questioned for some five hours and then released.

For months Joe and I dodged the bullet, but the heat was beginning to intensify. The feds had convened a grand jury investigation into the *Valhalla*. Under the tutelage of Captain Bob, our weak link held out under the initial barrage of questioning. But one night John McIntyre got stopped in Quincy for driving under the influence. I guess the local cops were scratching their heads when he started singing about one of Joe Murray's marijuana boats out in the harbor. I mean, they just arrested him for drunk driving! Sensing a jackpot, the Quincy police called customs. That night McIntyre confessed to being an IRA revolutionary who had just delivered seven tons of weapons to Ireland. He ratted everybody out.

Of course, Whitey found out about it right away. I cannot say for sure how Whitey found out the details. He never told any of us. All he said was that McIntyre was a rat who had to be dealt with immediately.

Joe Murray liked McIntyre and spoke to me about getting him out of the country until the *Valhalla*'s grand jury hearing was over. After all, McIntyre was a fantastic marine mechanic. He had been loyal to Joe for many years. He showed real courage during the weapons transfer and I respected that. I agreed with Murray and in no way wanted to see McIntyre harmed for ratting us out. He caved into the feds out of weakness, not malice. Unfortunately,

John McIntyre now had one major problem on his hands — Whitey Bulger.

One afternoon during this time Whitey and Kevin Weeks came to visit me at the gym. I'd just finished working out when I heard Kevin's voice. Whitey asked me to bring McIntyre to see him at my brother's house on East Third. Whitey told me they'd made the arrangements for McIntyre's departure to Spain. I never questioned him because Joe had already discussed the situation with me. I wished I would have called Joe before I found McIntyre. I got caught with my guard down.

McIntyre was working on one of Joe's boats in East Boston when he heard me walk up the plank. He wasn't a bit scared. Why should he be? He had no way of knowing Whitey knew about his conversation with the Quincy police. I let him know Whitey wanted to see him, and he took a few moments to wash the grease out from under his fingernails. On the ride back to Southie we discussed a new boat Joe was going to buy. He got a little apprehensive when my car stopped in front of my brother's house, but I reassured him things would be okay. I told him what I myself truly believed: that Whitey was just going to talk to him about going away for a little while until things cooled down.

Whitey, Stevie Flemmi, and Kevin Weeks were sitting in my brother's living room when McIntyre and I came through the front door. Whitey was wearing a tight black sweatshirt and a solid black baseball cap; he asked to speak to John alone in the kitchen. The living room got brighter when the kitchen light snapped on. But even at that moment I had no indication that something was deadly wrong.

Now, I fully understand that there are several other versions of what happened to John McIntyre. But this is how I remember it.

I had some business at the club and told them I'd be back. I returned to my brother's house an hour later. Nobody was in the living room or the kitchen. Whitey and Stevie called out to me from the cellar. When I reached the bottom step, I saw John McIntyre was face up on the dirt floor. His dungaree jacket was stained with blood and a rope was wrapped firmly around his neck. The chair he'd been sitting in was upright. I glanced over at Kevin — he appeared worried. There was a bullet wound in McIntyre's forehead but no great volume of blood on the floor.

Something had gone terribly wrong in that basement. John McIntyre had been tortured. He appeared to have been shot after he died. Most likely Whitey held the rope at one end while Stevie held the other. The sick bastards must have asked him questions while they yanked on the rope to cut off air at his windpipe. Stevie had a pair of pliers and was on his knees pulling out McIntyre's teeth; you could hear the teeth separating from the jawbone. Stevie's eyes held a glint of pleasure. He put each tooth in a small canvas bag, smashed the bag with a hammer, and then scattered the white powder around the floor. McIntyre's mouth wasn't filled with blood. The dead don't bleed like the living.

Whitey asked me to dig a five-foot hole to bury John right there in the cellar. He had to go upstairs and lie down; I figure that the release of sexual excitement from killing had exhausted him. Jimmy Bulger had climaxed in his pants. Whitey had had an orgasm while watching this young kid die.

I couldn't believe these guys had just killed this kid in my brother's house. I was enraged! They had killed John McIntyre, and they had done it in my brother's house!

But what do you do when you're in the room with two psychopaths who have just strangled a kid with a rope, shot him in the head, and pulled his teeth out with a set of pliers? Nobody with a fondness for living is going to say, "Hey, what the fuck did you guys do?" The most important thing for me to do at that moment was to contain my anger. I felt uneasy. I had no gun on me. What would it take for Whitey and Stevie to notice that I was not completely onboard? Not much, for these two paranoid psychos. So I had to do some disguising. I put on an attitude of "Hey, this is no big deal." Anything less would have been grounds for putting me in the hole next to McIntyre. Yes, it was that easy for guys like them.

I knew we were screwed now; the grand jury investigation had customs agents looking for McIntyre all over Boston. Whitey and Stevie drove McIntyre's car to the Pony Room, a well-known bar in Quincy. Joe Murray asked a lot of questions; he was concerned about John. I think he suspected something had gone wrong.

Of course, the feds came to me immediately. After all, I was the last one McIntyre had been seen with.

The federal authorities were steadily assembling the puzzle of the *Valhalla*. They were interrogating Captain Bob, Joe Murray, and me. I met with Whitey one night at the Mullen's Club, a small, little unlicensed hangout, and discussed the possibilities of my going away for a while. Things were getting too hot, and I knew it.

Whitey thought it was only a matter of time before the fallout from the *Valhalla* began to bring heat to our South Boston organization. At the time I had no idea how true those words really were. I knew Whitey was a rat, but I didn't know he'd given up the Angiulo brothers and my friend Howie Winter. In fact, that's how Whitey became the top Irish gangster in Boston: he ratted out Howie, and then took his place.

Anyway, Whitey and I put together a stash of money and a contingency plan in case things became too hot.

One morning shortly before we were indicted Whitey called me and asked me to meet him at Castle Island. He said he wanted to talk about the *Valhalla*, but I sensed differently. Whitey was wearing a Boston Red Sox cap and a tight white t-shirt. I walked with him for several minutes; neither of us spoke. He seemed to be collecting his thoughts.

"I got a deal with John Connolly," he spoke softly.

"What?" I heard him but couldn't believe those words had actually come out of his mouth. What a hypocrite; he hated rats. His whole life was about the code of silence, a criminal code of honor. I remember thinking, "He's set Irish criminals back a hundred years." But I couldn't do a thing. He was a sociopath. He'd already killed a dozen people. I was in trouble already with the *Marita Ann*'s capture. I had to think about my response — he could destroy me on the whole *Valhalla* thing.

The indictment came down on April 16, 1986. Joe Murray was grabbed first. The *Valhalla* had returned in October 1984; it took the feds almost sixteen months to get enough evidence to bring us down. Within an hour Whitey called to tell me that they had an arrest warrant for me, and I became a fugitive. Of course, he already knew.

I traveled first to Mexico and stayed in a safe house that belonged to Joe Murray. Joe owned lots of properties and used other people's names to hide assets. I stayed in Mexico for a month and then I came back to the States, to New Hampshire. Nobody knew me; I made up my history. Mostly I told people I'd retired from the military. A friend of mine from Southie, a "citizen," came out to spend time with me on the road.

Most of the time when you think of someone on the run you think of them being alone and miserable. But I was having a ball. Really. My friend and I modeled in a ski-clothing fashion show in Killington, Vermont. We had nothing but time. I trained every day either at the gym or outdoors, running or riding a bike, and got myself into great shape. Late that summer I began entering bike races. I actually raced in Concord, Massachusetts, under my own name. Basically I was living my life as I normally would, except I wasn't doing it in Southie.

I was hiding in plain sight, in New Hampshire or Massachusetts or Vermont, doing something that I had found I especially loved to do: race bicycles. Most of the time a local cop would be on duty keeping the traffic in check or holding back the spectators.

I was "on the lam," as Captain Bob would say, for about nine months, and that time raced by. I had an electronic pager, and Whitey called me whenever he thought I needed information. One day he called to tell me that the authorities were on their way to one of Joe Murray's houses in New Hampshire. I'd moved to Vermont, but Whitey didn't know that. I was starting to wonder if Whitey would give me up if he knew where I was.

I stayed in New England because of my family. I was back and forth to South Boston almost every month to see my daughters. I'd park a van at an appointed spot and the girls, ten and five at the time, would jump in the back. We'd eat at Kelly's Roast Beef or another place of their choice.

Every time I'd see my daughters I would know that I wasn't being the best dad possible, but this was the life I'd chosen a long time ago. My daughters thought it was a big deal, seeing their outlaw daddy. One night I pulled up in the van in the usual manner and my wife Debbie brought the girls out. (Debbie and I never did get divorced; we can't live together but we have always stayed good friends.) We went on a family vacation, our first one together in years. We spent a week in New Hampshire. It never crossed my mind that I was a fugitive. Debbie could have complained about putting the kids in jeopardy, but she never did; she was great. It was so good to just walk in the woods as a family. But, as happened every night since the *Marita Ann*'s capture, I would go to bed thinking, "I wish those guns had made it safely to Ireland."

By far the best adventure I had while on the run was the time I went to St. Louis for a Marine Corps anniversary dinner. I was surprised none of the police officers at Logan Airport recognized me. At the hotel in St. Louis, I knocked on the door of a Marine friend from South Boston. A Boston cop, he was quite startled to see me. Startled, but happy, because despite the fact that I was on the run, he was still a marine, an Irish American, and a solid Southie guy. To him what I'd done with the *Valhalla* was something he found not only acceptable but commendable.

My friend invited me to a dinner commemorating the Frozen Chosen, the marines who had fought in bitter, subzero conditions at the Chosin Reservoir during the Korean War. On November 27 and November 28, 1950, an estimated 120,000 Communist Chinese soldiers attacked some 20,000 Allied soldiers, including 17,000 men of the 1st Marine Regiment, sending them reeling in one of the most savage battles of modern warfare. It's been called the greatest fighting withdrawal in military history. (We Marines don't like to use the word *retreat*.)

It turned out that our old marine friend and Navy Cross recipient from Vietnam, James Webb, was the guest speaker at the dinner. At the time Jim was first assistant secretary of defense for Reserve affairs under President Reagan. (He later became secretary of the navy.) At the dinner I sat with another Southie guy, Tommy Lyons. We listened to stirring speeches and drank a few beers. Then I followed Tommy to the receiving line. Jim Webb spotted Tommy and me and pulled us aside.

"Pat, I understand you're underground."

"No, actually, I've turned myself in and I'm out on bail." I lied to him. But I had to; he was a government official. And he was my friend. I couldn't put him in jeopardy; I gave him deniability.

"I disagree with what you did with the weapons, but I understand your passion," he said, shaking my hand firmly.

I was apprehended a month later, on September 2, 1986, in Marshfield, Massachusetts. I'd actually been considering turning myself in. Joe Murray was trying to negotiate a deal. Captain Bob had almost been assured he would only get four years. They'd caught

an intellectual and fair judge who saw our political motivation —
something Margaret Thatcher never had the vision to see.

I'd gone to Marshfield to consult with my lawyer at his home.
He'd told me about the soft sentences the other guys might get
and I told him that I was ready to do the time and then get back
to a normal life. Well, "normal" for me anyway.

I'd been in Marshfield for about a week. It was a Sunday morning.
My son, Patrick, and his half-brother Jimmy Boyden had come to
meet me, and on a jog together I informed Patrick that things were
about to end — it was time for me to give myself up. But our conversation was cut short. We were coming down a sharp hill near a
church. An early mass was just about to end. I saw people heading
out the front door at about the same time I saw the cars surround us
— feds, local cops, and customs agents. Leave it to the customs
clowns: in their excitement to apprehend the big gunrunner they
didn't put their car in park and the car nearly rolled into several
unsuspecting churchgoers. They started to try to grab it — as if they
could hold a two-ton car from rolling down a hill. It was pretty comical. Classic for the customs team. Even the other cops smirked.

Then the fun was over. They separated Patrick and Jimmy from
me, but I learned they let the boys go after they questioned them
individually. Later Whitey told me that Jimmy Boyden had given
me up. But I told him to forget about it — I'd been planning to surrender that Monday anyway. I let him know I wanted nothing to
happen to Jimmy. "None of this McIntyre shit for Jimmy, Whitey.
You hear me?" I was firm and he saw the resolve in my eyes.

I found out later that the feds had planned my arrest to coincide
with Prince Charles' visit to Boston. He was speaking at Harvard
and the government wanted to make a statement about their commitment to stopping the IRA. But while I was waiting at the
Federal Building in Boston for what seemed like hours, more than
a couple of government types thanked me for what I'd done. Of
course, they all looked Irish American.

"Would you like some tea, Pat?" one of the FBI agents asked.

The customs agents were furious when the FBI guys removed my cuffs so that I could drink tea. They were furious for two reasons: one, this despicable gunrunner was being pampered with tea made by federal agents; and two, the FBI guys never even asked customs if they wanted anything. I could also hear the FBI guys who had been present at my arrest telling the other FBI guys about customs' runaway car. Boy, those customs clowns were pissed.

But I was done. I was placed under house arrest for nine months and then I pled guilty to smuggling arms. The judge was fair and gave me four years. If I had been caught today, under present gun-running laws, I'd be in Leavenworth for life and a day.

On June 12, 1987, my lawyer presented the following letter as an admission of my guilt.

DEFENDANT PATRICK NEE'S VERSION OF THE OFFENSE

In 1984, I became involved in efforts to acquire items which would be used to assist the oppressed Irish Catholics in Northern Ireland against the violent atrocities they were suffering at the hands of the British and Protestant authorities. At the time, I had overwhelming sympathies to the cause of the Irish Catholics and my history of participation in efforts to raise funds for the suffering families in Northern Ireland was well known in the community. Moreover, it is generally known that my training in the United States Marine Corps familiarized me with weapons and their accessories. The Statement of Facts in Support of Guilty Pleas to Information #1 (the Arms Offenses) prepared by the Government and submitted to this Court at the time of my entry of a guilty plea in this case in the main accurately describes the level of my participation in the offenses charged in this information. While I understood that the exportation of these materials to Ireland might violate the laws of the United States, I also believe that the acquisition of parts, accessories, training materials and ammunition from the various companies described in the information was not itself an illegal act. Indeed, most of these items were freely advertised in widely circulated publications and available by mail order. Moreover, I was also of the opinion that the United States Government has turned a blind eye to the acts of individuals attempting to assist oppressed people in various parts of the world who had no other means of support beyond that of sympathetic Americans. I do not intend for this explanation to minimize my awareness of the wrongfulness of my conduct, but I hope it will help the Court understand the motivation for said conduct.

I consider myself a loyal American, having served honorably in Vietnam and having devoted much of my time since then to assisting American veterans. However, having been born in Galway, Ireland, having maintained close contact with my family and friends in Ireland, and the harsh treatment of Catholics at the hands of the British, I have always had a sense of responsibility to these people from the land of my birth. Indeed, I have kept my home open to the children of Irish prisoners and have contributed my time and money on a regular basis to their cause. At no time have I sought any financial gain from my efforts on behalf of the Irish people and certainly do not reap any financial reward from my participation in the offenses to which I have pled guilty. I now know that I must confine my efforts in the future to offering financial assistance and supporting the political process which I hope will lead to the unification of Ireland and a future of freedom and democracy for the Irish people.

PATRICK NEE
June 12, 1987

They sent me to Danbury Federal Correctional Center in Connecticut to begin my sentence. I was housed with other men who all had one thing in common — the criminal gene. There were hit men, Mafiosi, and brilliant white-collar scam artists. We worked out together and told stories about our criminal lives. I did everything I could to occupy my time fully and to try to get out of prison early. I went to school, got my GED, and took some college courses — anything not to kill time, but to use it well. Seven months into my sentence my prison counselor came to me.

"Pat, I think you can make parole," he said.

"No way; it's too early. I'll never get it."

"I think you can. You have all these letters from teachers and a psychiatrist. You help everybody out. You're getting an education. You're a model inmate. Will you try if I put in for it?"

"Okay, but you're wasting your time," I replied.

Every six months the parole board met in the recreation room down by the gym. I stood in line for a good hour before it was my turn to go in. As the line moved closer I began to wish it would all work out in my favor. I went inside and saw two bureaucrats in suits. They sat at a folded table with stacks of files and a couple of Styrofoam coffee cups. They both had their heads down and were writing intensely on one page after another. I didn't think they knew I was in the room and that irritated me, so I cleared my throat.

"Patrick Nee," one spoke, "what have you accomplished in prison?"

He had the records right in front of him and I would have to assume he'd read them beforehand, but my bet was he had probably read the morning sports page instead.

"I've taken all the possible classes to improve myself."

"Do you stay in touch with the criminal associates from your past?"

"I don't," I said flatly, but honestly. Why would I? First, staying in touch with Whitey or anyone else would mean I wouldn't be sitting here at this moment. Plus, I was making all kinds of great criminal connections right there in Danbury. It was a silly question to ask someone who's surrounded by criminals, when you think about it.

I watched them read duplicates of my file. They showed no emotion as they skimmed the letters of recommendation. Their monotone voices seemed to become weaker — bored, really — with each question. But what amazed me was the fact that neither of them had yet looked at me.

"Well, since you have experienced this seven-month loss of freedom, if we granted you parole would you be inclined to continue the behavior that took that freedom from you?"

I didn't miss a beat.

"Yes, you can count on it."

One stopped writing — and had to fight the urge to look up at me.

"If the situation remains the same in Northern Ireland, I'll go back and finish my job," I said.

Both looked at me for the first time. All of a sudden I had their attention. My parole was denied and my poor counselor just walked away shaking his head. But I was honest — I would never compromise my principles.

I may be a criminal, but I am also an Irishman.